Enough Already

Winning Your Ugly
Struggle *with* Beauty

ENOUGH

ALREADY

Barbara L. Roose

ABINGDON PRESS
NASHVILLE

ENOUGH ALREADY
WINNING YOUR UGLY STRUGGLE WITH BEAUTY

Library of Congress Cataloging-in-Publication Data

Roose, Barbara.
  Enough already : winning your ugly struggle with beauty / Barbara Roose.
    pages cm
  Includes bibliographical references and index.
  ISBN 978-1-4267-8901-4 (binding: soft back,trade pbk. : alk. paper) 1. Christian women—Religious life. 2. Beauty, Personal—Religious aspects—Christianity. I. Title.
  BV4527.R645 2015
  248.8'43—dc23

                                                                    2014032765

15 16 17 18 19 20 21 22 23 24—10 9 8 7 6 5 4 3 2 1

MANUFACTURED IN THE UNITED STATES OF AMERICA

To all of the women who shared their beauty stories and struggles with me. You inspired this book, and I dedicate it to you.

CONTENTS

CONTENTS

ACKNOWLEDGMENTS

Special thanks to Lee Powell, the elders, and staff at Cedar Creek Church for many years of love and support. Lee, thank you for creating a platform for me to learn and grow under your leadership.

To my "go-to girls"—Ladies, we've been through so much over the years. Thank you for the treasure of your friendship and loving me along the way.

To Rachelle Gardener —You've been an answer to so many of my prayers. Thank you for creating space for me to access your wisdom and expertise.

To Pamela Clements—Thank you for believing in me and this project. Your advice and guidance has been invaluable.

Sandie Bricker—God delivered you into my life at just the right place and the right time. You've blessed me in so many ways!

Amanda Roose and Shelley Adams—Thank you both for being my gladiators while I prepared the book for submission. Your sacrifice for this project as well as your input and expertise meant so much.

Mom and Dad—No one could be luckier than me to have parents like you.

Kate, Samantha, and Abigail—You are beautiful. And I am so thankful that I am your mom.

Finally, Matt—Thank you for standing by my side as we've fought through some of life's ugly moments to find the beauty in each other every day. I love you.

INTRODUCTION

Give a woman a mirror and thirty seconds, and she'll tell you everything that is wrong with how she looks.

Is that statement true for you? When you look in the mirror, what do you say about your face, skin, hair, or stomach? How long does it take for you to look in a mirror and start listing all of the things about yourself that you wish you could change?

Every woman, regardless of age, struggles at some level with what she sees in the mirror. I call this our "ugly struggle with beauty." The core of this struggle isn't about clothing size, body shape, or fashion style. This struggle isn't about a diet or exercise plan. Ladies, our ugly struggle with beauty is a battle over our God-given identity in a world that wants us to believe that beauty is a prize only a few women can claim.

Although we know that inner beauty trumps physical beauty, I've discovered that both types of beauty must interact with each other. Yes, what's on the inside matters most, but it's not the only thing that matters.

Enough Already addresses the origins of our ugly struggle with beauty as well as how to equip ourselves to win the battle and claim our God-given beauty. It doesn't matter if you are single, married, or single again, there are things that you need to know about how God created you to be His expression of beauty in our world. You weren't created to look in the mirror and sigh with disappointment. Even if life has tried to steal your beauty, you'll discover that what God has given you cannot be taken away. As you discover what it means to cultivate your God-given beauty, you'll mount a defense and win your ugly struggle once and for all!

This book contains lots of stories about my ugly struggle with beauty. You'll find out why Barbie dolls were the bane of my existence as well as why I almost stopped smiling. As my knowledge and experience with God has grown, I can now see how He has redeemed those difficult and painful moments in my life. I can also smile as I've been blessed by the opportunity to share my journey with you. I hope that my stories and insights give you reason to smile and know that you are beautiful just because you are created by God.

Together, we are going to take the topic of beauty from something that you try to buy for $10.99 (with a coupon!) and reframe our understanding of it through God's eyes. We'll work to eliminate the fear that we're not skinny enough, curvy enough, or tall enough and discover that God's best is already within us. This is a journey that can heal our painful battle wounds that too many of us have sustained in this ugly struggle.

My friend, no matter where you find yourself spiritually these days, I will trust and believe that God will make His presence known to you during your journey. I pray that you will experience His presence during this journey. I also pray that God reveals the deepest origins of the ugly struggle with beauty and heals those wounded places with His love and truth.

Finally, I pray that God will send you other women—maybe even new friends—to share this experience as well. This isn't a journey that anyone should make alone.

In Jesus' name, we can do this together and discover that in God's eyes, you are enough, already!

OUR UGLY STRUGGLE WITH BEAUTY

At that moment their eyes were opened, and they suddenly felt shame at their nakedness.

—Genesis 3:7

All I wanted to do that night was buy a new outfit. Instead, my department store dressing room turned into a battle zone.

I was running errands on a Wednesday night and decided to stop by Kohl's for a little retail therapy. It hadn't been a good day—you know, the kind of day when nothing seems to go right. I strolled to the front door, hoping that an hour of wandering in and out of the various clearance sections could improve my mood. Clearance prices always make me smile.

At first, the clearance-rack mojo seemed to be swinging to my beat. First, I discovered a long, swingy black sweater dress that was 70 percent off. A few racks later, I delicately fingered a lovely cream top, also on clearance. Then, my gaze fell upon a pair of black pleather pants in my size. I've never, ever tried on pleather or its genuine leather cousin, yet I heard an odd little voice in my brain whispering, "You have a gift card and a 20-percent-off coupon. Try them on."

Now, I'm 5′10″, and my weight is roughly the equivalent of a skinny supermodel strapped down with a few healthy two-year-olds. I'm a curvy girl—on the top and bottom—with long legs. All of this means that trying on pants in the best of circumstances is often an ordeal.

Then, there's the *two* servings of cheesy orzo pasta I ate for dinner.

As women, we must accept many unsavory realities about store dressing rooms. We deal with harsh lighting and big mirrors, and we pretend not to remember there is some guy in a hidden room sitting in front of dozens of monitors as cameras watch our every move. Even if dude in the camera room happens to be a creeper, he still isn't our biggest problem in the dressing room. Our biggest issue resides in the brain space between our ears.

My dressing room odysseys are hardly rational. There's something that happens when I disrobe and become vulnerable in the large mirror in front of me. The way those clothes fit suddenly becomes some type of statement about who I am. For example: If I grab a pair of jeans in my regular size, but they cling in the leg or hips, all of a sudden, I believe that my rear is too big. Conversely, if I slip into a dress that makes me feel like a rock star, I look in the mirror and the little voice in my head tells me that I am wonderful and invincible—and that I can scarf down a few extra cookies at snack time.

Unfortunately, those pleather pants fell into the first category. Sigh. *I lost again.*

Whenever I cross over the threshold into the dressing room, the battle begins. The opponents in this battle never change: ME versus ME. There's the ME in my mind pitted against the ME that I see in the mirror. Too often, it's a lopsided battle because the ME in my mind sabotages the ME in the mirror.

It's crazy and embarrassing for me to admit these things. But I comfort myself in thinking that you might be a little crazy, too.

A few years ago, I bought full-length mirrors for each of my daughters at Walmart for $5 each. I was supposed to mount the mirrors on the wall next to their closets, but the girls decided they would rather lean the mirrors against the wall. I have a large, fancy mirror in my room. But I don't like my mirror. I like theirs. In fact, I've been known to finish dressing and double-check myself in their mirrors instead of mine. Why? Their mirrors make me look taller and thinner. I also feel prettier. How is that even true? I don't know, and I don't care. All I know is that when I look into the mirror, what I see has an impact on how I feel about myself.

Here's a challenge for you: find a mirror and hold it up to your face. Can you repeat the following without flinching: "I'm beautiful"? Repeat it: "I'm beautiful."

How do those words feel as they come out of your mouth? Do you feel like you are talking about yourself, or do you feel disconnected from those words? If you can't even say them, it's OK. You're not alone.

NUMBERS DON'T LIE

What is *beauty*? Dictionary.com defines *beauty* as a "quality present in a thing or person that gives intense pleasure or deep satisfaction to the mind."[2] Look at that definition once more. Do you realize that nowhere in the definition of *beauty* are the words *perfection* or *flawless*? Yet that seems to be what we've elevated our expectation of beauty to be. When I reflect on this definition, I understand why many women don't consider themselves beautiful. We don't find our appearance pleasurable, and when we consider our entire external person, we are far from satisfied.

Dove's 2004 Campaign for Real Beauty provided a wake-up call to women regarding to the topic of beauty. At the time, the company's survey revealed that a whopping 98 percent of women did not believe that they were beautiful. In 2011, Dove released an additional set of findings, and the percentage of women who believed they were beautiful was adjusted from 2 percent to 4 percent.[1]

My degree is in English, which means my math skills are mediocre at best. Yet, I am crazy awesome at calculating store discounts. Really, it's a gift. So, here is a shopping analogy: if Macy's had your favorite shoe or sneaker for 96 percent off, you might be tempted to act a little less than ladylike for some of that action. Although a 96-percent discount on shoes is worthy of celebration, that same 96 percent signals that we have an epic tragedy on our hands when it comes to whether or not we approve of our self-image.

Many women will admit to having beautiful eyes or a beautiful smile. We might admit that we think our legs or hair is beautiful. However, it is a rare woman who can confidently stand up to say: "My name is _____ and I'm beautiful." Who is brave enough to admit to complete beauty, not just a partial, conditional beauty? Sadly, 96 percent of us feel that we cannot do that.

Why is it so hard to stand in front of a full-length mirror and smile comfortably and confidently at what we see—and perhaps even cheer? One of my favorite parts of being a woman is that we love to shop one another's bodies. We smile and lavish compliments such as, "What a lovely shirt!" "Honey, I love those shoes!" or "Your hair looks wonderful." We love telling our girlfriends when they look beautiful. Yet, that is a graciousness that we would never extend to ourselves.

WHERE OUR UGLY STRUGGLE BEGAN

Our ugly struggle with beauty has its origins in the garden of Eden. Once upon a time, Adam and Eve were created and placed in the most perfect place on earth. God's perfect touch crafted bodies that were divinely beautiful, not based on a particular size, shape, or Photoshop skill.

Did you ever think about how Eve felt about her body? Check out Genesis and read about Eve's life in the garden of Eden. Notice that Eve experienced no angst, no disillusionment over her physical appearance. I wonder if Eve had that coveted gap between her knees. When Eve looked down at her arms, legs, breasts, and thighs, there were no groans or sighs, only peace and contentment. Can you imagine that?

Adam and Eve enjoyed unbridled access to the beauty and perfection of the garden as well as the freedom to consume its bounty. There was only one exception: the Tree of the Knowledge of Good and Evil. Here are God's instructions to Adam and Eve in Genesis 2:16-17: "You may freely eat the fruit of every tree in the garden—except the tree of the knowledge of good and evil. If you eat its fruit, you are sure to die."

In Genesis 3, we read about a serpent who engages in a twisting, manipulative dialogue with an unwitting Eve. The serpent began with questioning Eve's knowledge of God's instructions about the *do*s and *don't*s in the garden of Eden.

All it took for Eve to flip on God's instructions in favor of the serpent was a little pushback. The serpent appealed to Eve's pride, and that's all it took. I've always wondered why Eve seemed to fold so easily. Then again, I'm the woman whose emotional self-worth can be taken down by a pair of ill-fitting jeans.

It is in Genesis 3 that our ugly struggle with beauty begins. Eve was deceived by the serpent, and when her eyes were opened, she scampered to cover her body. When God came to visit Adam and Eve in the evening, their recognition of their naked bodies was evidence of their shame.

Perhaps it is no coincidence that the word *shame* used in Genesis 3 is the same word that far too many women use to describe their current attitude toward themselves.

And where there is shame, we struggle to find beauty.

THE PAIN OF OUR STRUGGLES

There is more to life than being able to proclaim our beauty in front of the bathroom mirror. Yes, our value as women shouldn't depend on a bathroom scale or clothing size. But let's not pretend that those things aren't important. Let's stop shooing away the topic of outer beauty like a bothersome fly at a picnic. Let's admit that how we feel about what we see in the mirror does matter. It's not the only thing that matters, but it does matter.

A few weeks before Christmas, I visited with a friend I've known for years. Her ex-husband made some plans for his life that didn't include her. This friend has courageously carved out a life as a single mother and worked to overcome the pain of her past.

As we sipped chai tea at my dining room table, my friend bravely admitted that she has never felt beautiful, and as a result, she lessened her expectations of how her husband should treat her. "I've never been beautiful. I'm not even sure I would describe myself as attractive. It's OK because I accepted that about myself when I was in high school. In fact, when my husband and I married, I was relieved because I thought he was marrying me for who I was on the inside and not because of what I looked like on the outside."[3]

My heart hurt for my friend as I listened to her painful story. Here is a loving, compassionate woman who did not believe that she is beautiful.

Ladies, our ugly struggle with beauty is a war on two fronts: against our culture and against ourselves. Although we cannot control the media or the messages it creates, we are 100 percent in control of our beliefs, responses, and choices when it comes to the topic of beauty. Our goal is to learn how to push back against society and self-deception.

During our journey together, we need to remember that God is the Creator of beauty, and as women, we were created to be the standard-bearers of His beauty in this world. When we see ourselves through this filter, we can fight back and triumph over our ugly struggle with beauty.

BEAUTY MARK
Where there is shame, we will struggle to find beauty.

GROUP DISCUSSION QUESTIONS

You can use these questions in a small group format or talk about them over coffee or lunch with a friend or an accountability partner. You don't have to answer all questions; just choose the ones that are most meaningful for your group.

1. Are you surprised that 96 percent of women don't think they're beautiful? Are you part of the 96 percent or the 4 percent?

2. How are you impacted by our culture's obsession with outer beauty?

3. Are you more comfortable talking about the facets of inner beauty (virtue, strength, or integrity) or the facets of outer beauty (clothes, makeup, fashion, and so on)?

4. If you completely ignore your appearance, can you list some reasons why? If you feel that you are obsessed with or spend too much time on your appearance, can you list some reasons why?

5. Have you ever thought about Eve's life in the garden of Eden before being deceived by the serpent? How would your life be different if all of the concern, angst, or misery over your appearance disappeared?

PERSONAL JOURNALING QUESTIONS

Each chapter is designed to strike deep into the tension between inner and outer beauty. While you can and should receive important feedback from others during the group discussion time, this journaling section should be between you and God. Invite Him into this portion of the experience, and use the space provided to record any reflections or impressions you are thinking or feeling.

1. How do you feel about yourself?

2. What do you like about yourself?

3. When do you feel the most secure about yourself?

4. When do you feel the most insecure?

WHO TOLD US THAT
WE WEREN'T BEAUTIFUL?

"You won't die!" the serpent replied to the woman. "God knows that your eyes will be opened as soon as you eat it, and you will be like God, knowing both good and evil." The woman was convinced.
—*Genesis 3:4-6a*

Do you look at the magazines in the checkout area at the market? I do. I like looking at the pictures of the pretty dresses. Those colorful magazine covers lure us in with attention-grabbing titles. Here are a few of the front cover titles from just one magazine:

> "How to Look Sexy at 30, 40, 50, & 60"
> "Got Belly Fat? We'll Convince You to Lose It"
> "The Whole Body Anti-aging Guide"[1]

Now, to be fair, these weren't the only titles on the cover; there was also a small headline about setting a pretty table for Thanksgiving.

When we see titles about how to lose weight or look sexy, there is a subtle message that we are not good enough as we are. If we hear enough of those messages and believe them, then we will also believe that our only choice is to seek out the solutions that our culture provides—for a price. But after we pay the price, our culture introduces a new flaw, a new area of insecurity designed to bring us back for yet another solution. All of a sudden we find ourselves on a hamster wheel that spins and spins, with millions of women trying to keep up on the inside. I don't know about you, but I'm tired of trying to keep up.

DO YOU FEEL THE PRESSURE?

The beauty industry generates $50 billion in annual sales in the United States.[2] Women are obviously the biggest consumers of beauty products. So, in order to keep those company profits rolling, marketing has to appeal to women in a way that elicits a buying reaction.

Now, as one who chips in her fair portion toward that $50 billion each year, I'm not villainizing the beauty industry, which has blessed me in many ways. Without facial cleanser, my skin would look like it was still trapped in adolescence. Without skin creams, my arms and legs would be flaky and ashy. Hair dyes hide the gray, and we all know why razors are important. I appreciate beauty products and the way they enhance my quality of life.

However, we do have to realize that the beauty industry's financial survival depends on whether we will buy its products at the prices it sets. We have to be wise enough to recognize that in order for the industry to make money, it must convince us that we need its products. One of the ways this happens is to create an unreasonable standard and to pressure us to chase after that standard.

CREATED WITH CURVES SURVEY

Beauty is one of those topics that always generates a lot of discussion. However, the places where we struggle with beauty can be filled with pain, so we may not be as willing to talk about them. I launched my *Created with Curves* survey in September 2013 to gather feedback from women about a variety of beauty-related topics. Not only did more than five hundred women anonymously give their opinions, but they also shared their precious stories.[3]

One of my questions was, "How much pressure do you feel to fit our culture's definition of beauty?" Here are the results:

Extreme pressure—8 percent
A lot of pressure—39 percent
Some pressure—48 percent
No pressure—5 percent

What about you? How much pressure did you or do you feel to look a certain way? Here are two responses from the *Created with Curves* survey:

When I was younger, I was very thin and flat chested. Even my mother-in-law made a comment that she didn't know what first attracted her son to me because I didn't have a womanly shape. I considered having breast implants for a long time. . . .[4]

I struggle with accepting my aging body. I am painfully aware that as I age I am being compared to much younger women. Right now as I am taking this survey, I am at a salon getting my grey roots covered. I would love to drop the facade and go natural but don't think the impact would be good for my career.[5]

I applaud these women for being honest in the survey about the pressure they feel to be beautiful. Personally, I checked "some pressure." For me, that's an improvement! After working in sales for a few years and dealing with my own beauty baggage for many more, I can happily say that I feel less pressure than before. But yes, sometimes I feel pressure to buy certain products or try to look a certain way.

THE SNAKE IN OUR SKIN CREAM

Years ago, *Saturday Night Live* character Enid Strict, otherwise known as "the Church Lady," touted her foolish brand of self-righteous wisdom to elicit laughs from the audience. At least once during her weekly skit, she would ask: "Could it be Satan?" The audience waited for that line each week and then howled with laughter every time, as if Satan couldn't possibly be responsible for creating havoc in their lives.[6]

Although some of you may not have any particular spiritual background, you must understand that our ugly struggle with beauty is more than skin deep. It's a battle waged in our hearts, minds, and souls. This struggle is part of a spiritual war that began in the garden of Eden when the serpent deceived Eve into eating the fruit. This serpent is also known as Satan.

Talking about Satan in a book about beauty might seem like dropping an axe on a toothpick, but trust me, ladies, Satan is behind our ugly struggle with beauty. If everything that God created is good and Satan is the enemy of God, then Satan's endgame is to degrade and destroy everything that God created—including us.

When it comes to our ugly struggle with beauty, we have to realize that there is a snake slithering about in our skin cream. This isn't a skit on a weekend television show. There is no punch line. This time, no one is laughing.

I'm not saying that Satan is behind products created by the beauty industry. Lipstick, mani-pedis, designer purses, and fabulous stilettos are neither bad nor good. What we need to examine are the evil messages that tempt us to believe that we could never be beautiful.

Some of you are uncomfortable talking about Satan. You may not even be completely convinced that he exists. Although I know it's uncomfortable bringing Satan into our discussion at the beginning of our journey, we need to flip on this light because for too long Satan has figured out how to fool us and how to manipulate our culture while never letting us see his ugly nature.

My precious friend, Satan's deepest desire is for you to be discouraged and to give up on ever believing that God created you beautiful. Instead, he wants you to look in the mirror and feel disdain or discouragement. Satan knows that when you feel those crushing emotions, you will experience shame. When we live with shame, we draw inward, and God cannot use us to make a beautiful impact in our world.

As much as Satan is responsible for deceiving and discouraging, our world has been caught up in the pursuit of a form of beauty that is far from God's original intent. The scriptural author, the Apostle Paul, cautions us to be aware of man-made standards. Pay attention to the following warning in Colossians 2:8: "Don't let anyone capture you with empty philosophies and high-sounding nonsense that come from human thinking and from the spiritual powers of this world, rather than from Christ."

Our world wants us to seek for satisfaction in what I like to call "faux beauty" or "fake beauty." Faux beauty might sound fancy, but a fake is a fake.

IS FAKE THE NEW REAL?

One day I strolled through the doors of a local retail store, trolling for some bargains. Yes, trolling, as in, "This girl ain't too proud to dig through the sales racks to look for something fabulous at a great price." I asked the sales associate to pull down an interesting-looking vest hanging from a hook high above so that I could have a closer look. The black vest's contour had classic lines, but the zipper and the embellishments had a funky style that I immediately loved.

The nice young man at the cash register stroked his fingers over the vest and smiled at me. "Don't you just love this vest?"

I smiled back. "I absolutely do."

Then, he continued: "So, do you know why I love this vest so much?"

(I didn't say anything back because he really wasn't looking at me. He was going to tell me anyway, whether I wanted to know or not.)

"This vest is vegan leather. Isn't that so cool?"

As my chatty sales clerk kept talking, I discovered that vegan leather wasn't a new kind of leather; it was just a fancy term for what I grew up calling "pleather," as in, "Don't get caught dead on the playground wearing pleather shoes." Yet, he talked about the "vegan leather" material as if it was the answer to all of my couture hopes and dreams.

I didn't care about whether the vest was leather or pleather. It was cute. It was my size. I wanted to buy it. I wanted to tell the nice young man, "Look, don't try to make me believe that something is real when it isn't."

Does it matter to you if something is real or fake? These days, fake eyelashes are hot. I received two sets of free fake eyelashes as part of a beauty subscription box. I haven't worn them yet. The thought of gluing something next to my eyeball sends me into a panic. Any foolish attempt to apply that gluey little strip to my eyelid is a trip to the emergency room just waiting to happen. "Ma'am, can you tell me again, exactly how did you glue your eyelid shut?"

Isn't it amazing how technology makes "fake" seem like it is real? Each week, I read articles about magazines that digitally alter photos of celebrities and models. The digital technicians trim, lengthen, lighten, highlight, smooth, contour, or erase away anything that won't fulfill the illusion of perfection. My heart goes out to actresses and models who see these altered images of themselves plastered on magazine covers or billboards. Can you imagine posing for a photo and then seeing the final image so drastically changed that it no longer looks like you, but your name is on it? Furthermore, imagine the pressure of having to live up to that faux image because that is what people expect when they see you live and in person at the neighborhood store or movie premiere.

We live in a world surrounded by images that look real but are not. Yet, they are marketed to us as the reality we should embrace. In our image-driven world, one of Satan's strategies is to overwhelm us with those images so that we might embrace the faux beauty marketed to us.

The Apostle Paul gives the following advice to believers to guide and encourage them in a world that wanted to destroy them. In the context of our discussion, Colossians 3:2 reminds us of where to focus: "Think about the things of heaven, not the things of earth."

God desires for us to prioritize thinking about what is true and everlasting. The images before us in magazines and Instagram photos are as fleeting as yesterday's news. Those things come and go, but God's truth about who we are and our purpose on this earth never changes. When we keep our eyes on the things of heaven, we see those digitally created images for what they are, and therefore their impact is lessened. Those images are not evil, but we know that they are fake and that our value in God's eyes is real so that we do not have to strive to live up to a fake image.

There are some things in life that must be authentic. Our desire for beauty must be one of them. As we continue our journey together, commit yourself to discovering the true beauty God has already created you to be. Sure, we're always going to have to deal with magazine covers, lingerie advertisements, and anyone younger, skinnier, taller, or curvier than we are. But don't ever let yourself be led astray by someone else's beauty rules.

BEAUTY MARK
Satan's desire is to deceive you into believing that you can never be beautiful.

GROUP DISCUSSION QUESTIONS

1. What are some of the funniest or silliest beauty-related promises you've seen on the front of magazines?

2. When you see article titles such as "Be Sexier" or "Be Thinner" on those magazine covers, which ones attract your interest more?

3. When do you feel the most amount of pressure to fit our culture's standard of beauty? How would you describe how that pressure feels?

4. Does it seem strange to you that we would involve Satan in our discussion about beauty? Why do you think it is important to recognize his role behind the scenes of our ugly struggle with beauty?

5. What are some of the ways that our culture has replaced God's standards for human ones? What has been the result?

PERSONAL JOURNALING QUESTIONS

1. How do you feel when you see the women on the magazine covers? Yes, we know that many of those photos are enhanced, but how to you feel about them?

2. How has the pressure to look a certain way affected your life? Are you angry or sad about the fact that you feel that pressure?

3. When do you feel that you are not beautiful?

4. Think about the idea that Satan is behind the scenes working to convince you that you are not beautiful. How can Satan use a magazine cover or beauty advertisement to do real harm to your heart and soul?

WHAT IS YOUR BEAUTY NARRATIVE?

It was by faith that Rahab the prostitute was not destroyed with the people in her city who refused to obey God.

—Hebrews 11:31

I'll never forget the day when a woman came up to me and said, "No, you could never be on a magazine cover. Your face features don't work; your eyes are small, you have a small face but a big nose." I was only 14, and I had never noticed any of that stuff, you know?[1]

—Gisele Bündchen, supermodel

It's hard to believe that anyone could have ever said anything negative about supermodel Gisele Bündchen's face or body. However, Gisele is not immune to the inner struggle regarding beauty that we all must manage. Look at her words above and notice how her quote begins with the phrase: "I'll never forget . . ."

Think about the defining moments you've experienced in your family of origin, at school, or in the workplace. How have those defining moments shaped your relationship with the topic of inner or outer beauty? These experiences are all a part of your personal beauty narrative.

If we are not observant at the onset or reflective in the conclusion, we may go for years without realizing that a story line is being created and miss the impact that the plot has on our heart, mind, and behavior. It is amazing how an ongoing story of related or unrelated events, situations, and statements coagulates and then crystallizes in our hearts and minds. The collection of story lines becomes our beauty narrative and impacts what we think about ourselves or how others see us. Most important, we should not think that the evolution of our beauty narrative ends when we become adults. Too often, we ignore defining moments during our adult years that create disharmony in our relationship with inner and outer beauty.

Do any of the following statements describe words or phrases you've heard in your lifetime?

"Pretty girls like you should have anything they want."
"Fatty-fatty, two-by-four, can't get through the kitchen door."
"Your skin's so dark, you'd disappear at night."
"You're so ugly that (fill-in-the-blank)."

Our beauty narratives are a mixture of positive and negative events and circumstances. Here is some insight into my childhood beauty narrative:

Once upon a time, there was a little girl named Barbara Louise. Young Barbara loved to ride her pink bike up and down the sidewalk and watch cartoons. Most of all, little Barbara loved to gather together with her favorite little girl cousins to play with their dolls. Each afternoon, the little girls gathered to travel into a magical dreamland with the most perfect doll of them all . . .

I've lived my life in the shadow of a creature known for her flawless perfection and radiant beauty. Although not as popular now as in years past, she was once worshiped by millions of little girls and grown women around the world. Although dozens of wannabes have emerged looking to claim a share of her former glory, her reign as the greatest of all time continues. Even though she never failed to maintain her perfect smile and innocent gaze, her presence taunted me as a child, but I couldn't say why. Her name: Barbie.

When I was a child, Barbie dolls were everywhere. Little girls adored the eleven-and-a-half-inch tall plastic doll with an anatomically impossible skinny waist, long blonde hair, doe-shaped eyes, freakishly long eyelashes, silky straight (and static-prone) hair, and an enviable arched foot. My cousins and I would dress our Barbie dolls in luxurious, shiny polyester gowns with Velcro zippers and stiletto plastic heels. We dreamed that our dolls had high-paying jobs, lived in palatial estates, and came home every night to handsome husband Ken. In our eyes, since Barbie was beautiful, she had to be rich. Our dolls were living out fantasies that we hoped existed in reality. In our immature eyes, those Barbie dolls were perfect—and perfection meant that anything was possible.

During our playtime, there was always a moment when at least one of my cousins would point out that, even though I shared Barbie's name, I looked nothing like her. And I agreed. I was a quiet, brown-skinned little girl with large, round glasses and big front teeth. I often wondered how I could share a name with a creation so perfect. You see, as a little girl, I hoped that I could be many things when I grew up, but beautiful would never be one of them. Since our quartet of giggly girls agreed that Barbie was beautiful and I didn't look like Barbie, the pages of my beauty narrative opened, and the first line went something like this: "Since I do not look like the pretty Barbie dolls, then I cannot be pretty. If I am not pretty, then I should not dream of all of the things that pretty little girls should dream about."

Every woman has a beauty narrative. Most of them remain unspoken until we sense that there is a safe place to release our summation. Yet, whether those beauty narratives remain spoken or unspoken, they still impact our lives.

Sometimes, I'll hear a woman brag about how beautiful she is—and how other women should be envious of her looks. As much as I want to accept her statement as genuine, I cannot help but wonder about her beauty narrative and what kinds of statements, circumstances, or events she has absorbed and converted into such brassy proclamations. I wonder whether beneath the bold words there is a beauty narrative filled with circumstances that were the opposite of what she wants us to think.

Here is one powerful story shared by a *Created with Curves* survey participant reflecting a beauty narrative that still impacts her life today:

> As an incest survivor, I was told that I was ugly and fat and would never amount to anything, and I have believed that in my heart my whole life.
>
> I worked my tail off in high school to get thin, but it didn't make me happy, and I was still called "the great white whale" after losing over fifty pounds eating cheddar cheese, cucumbers, and Diet 7-Up for months.
>
> Today, I am close to four hundred pounds; my body is a time bomb; I need hip replacements. I lost my parents to diabetes, and I am now diabetic as well. I am dying in the same ugly way my parents did. I can't make myself stop eating because I know it won't make me happier. Now that I am also blind, I can't use makeup because I would have it everywhere, and I've had one haircut in five years because I can't afford to have it cut.

I know that what I was told as a child shouldn't still affect
me as a 47-year-old woman, but once it is drilled into your
head over and over and over, it becomes too real to fight.

Some of you know exactly how she feels. You've struggled with a
statement or event that happened to you long ago, and in quiet moments, that narrative sneaks in and hijacks your hope, your peace, and
any attempt you make at seeing yourself as beautiful.

What you need to know is that those whispering thoughts are not
the truth about who you are. Those thoughts might be a memory, but
they are not your reality. That narrative does not define who you are!

BEAUTY NARRATIVES
FOR CHRISTIAN WOMEN

As a Christian woman who has struggled with the topic of beauty, I
believe that evaluating our individual beauty narratives is essential to
living in God's truth regarding our existence as His beloved creation.
Unfortunately, we live in a fallen world, and what we hear, see, and experience is often a reflection of our sinful nature.

If that is the case, then why does the topic of outer beauty produce a
weary sigh among Christian women? Why should we dismiss the opportunity to have a legitimate conversation about how our inner beauty and
outer beauty can—and should—intersect and complement each other?

Over the years, I have received numerous invitations to speak about
the topic of beauty. It's a topic that all women care about. However, I
noticed that my talks were about the inner qualities of beauty, but the
conversations that women were having with one another were about
worries over physical beauty. There was a tremendous disconnect, yet
no one wanted to admit it.

For some reason, we've deemed it unspiritual to talk about beauty.
Yet we harbor all kinds of secret language and beliefs.

Here are some common statements from beauty narratives of Christian women:

> "God only cares about my heart, not what I look like."
> "Doesn't the Bible say that charm is deceitful and beauty is vain?"
> "Only vain women care about hair and makeup."
> "If I am vocal about my desire to dress or look attractive, people may not think I am truly a Christian."

I hope that you are willing to think through, even write down, the beauty narratives that have impacted your life. There are messages that you've absorbed about how you look, and those messages must be held up in the light of God's truth. Your life story may not read like a fairy tale, but trust me, friend, God can change any narrative.

RAHAB'S NEW NARRATIVE

Rahab was a prostitute in the Old Testament. We don't know much about her life, but the word *prostitute* fills in a lot of blanks. Chances are, she was shunned by her community and her family was ashamed of her occupation. This was probably not what Rahab hoped that she would grow up to be; but in ancient society, an unmarried woman, like a widow with no male relatives to care for her, would often turn to prostitution in order to survive.

Imagine that you are Rahab. Imagine the words you hear each day from the men who use you or the women who sneer at you while you shop in the marketplace or do laundry in the river. Day after day, Rahab was inundated with negative statements about who she was and what she did. Of course, in the quiet moments between customers, Rahab would undoubtedly repeat those same things to herself: "I am worthless" or "This is all I ever will be."

In Joshua 2, there were some Israelite spies doing some advance scouting around the town of Jericho, following God's direction. We don't know how the men ended up at Rahab's home. We don't know if they realized that she was a prostitute. All we know is that Rahab protected the men from certain death—even misleading the king of Jericho to save their lives. As a result of her interactions with those spies, Rahab's narrative takes a radical twist.

In Joshua 6, Israelite leader Joshua comes back to rescue Rahab and her family. He saves them from the slaughter happening in the city of Jericho. Since Scripture repeatedly refers to her as "Rahab the prostitute," there was no doubt that Joshua knew who he was saving. It must have been quite heady for Rahab to flee the carnage in Jericho by stepping over the slain bodies of the men and women who had called her names and made her feel ugly on the inside and out.

Rahab's story line is not mentioned again in the Old Testament. We don't know about her life after being rescued, but in the early New Testament, we discover her name in Jesus' lineage—she probably would have never seen that coming! Then, we cross paths with Rahab again in Hebrews 11, a chapter known as the "Hall of Faith" in the Bible. Rahab's act of faith was specifically called out in a chapter filled with the heroic acts of faith of key Old Testament leaders and countless, nameless God worshipers. Even though her early beauty narrative was filled with ugly experiences, God redeemed Rahab's life and wrote her a new narrative, one filled with honor and legacy.

My friend, I don't know your beauty narrative or the impact that it has had on your life. Surely, we all have some messages that have nicked and wounded our souls. Yet God has a beauty narrative waiting for you—a story line in which you are treasured and valued for who He has created you to be.

BEAUTY MARK
No matter the early chapters of your life story, God's narrative for your life includes beauty and purpose.

GROUP DISCUSSION QUESTIONS

1. What are some of the beauty narratives that have had an impact on your life?

2. Sometimes, women are reluctant to admit that there are still some beauty narratives that sting. Often, we pretend that the damage doesn't exist when it really does. What is the harm in ignoring or denying harmful beauty narratives?

3. Barb shared how her name and Barbie dolls impacted her beauty narrative. What were some of the people and experiences that impacted your beauty narrative?

4. The beauty of Rahab's story is that, even though there was a lot of ugly, one important twist in her life story changed everything. No matter how you feel about yourself or your beauty narrative, name something that you are proud of or a facet of your personality that blesses or nurtures others.

PERSONAL JOURNALING QUESTIONS

1. Is there any memory or other thought that has surfaced as a result of this chapter? Just make a note of it as well as how you feel about it now and any reflections you might have now.

2. What are the positive beauty narratives that you have experienced? When did you hear or experience them, and how have they impacted your life?

3. Are there any beauty narratives that are severely damaging how you see yourself? How has that narrative hurt or harmed you?

FLAW FINDING

> *Guard your heart above all else,*
> *for it determines the course of your life.*
> —*Proverbs 4:23*

One day, I took my then five-year-old daughter, Abbie, shopping with me to pick up a few things at the store. Like her sisters, Abbie has a kind and loving heart, and I can always count on her to have something sweet and supportive to say to me.

As we entered into the dressing room with the morning's selection, I realized there was no bench for Abbie to sit on outside of the room close by, so I settled her on the little corner perch inside the room and locked the door.

Promising to be quick, I handed Abbie some crackers and turned to disrobe. Since the dressing room can be a judgment room, I'm sure I was getting mentally prepared for trying on those clothes. I heard munching in the background as I turned away from Abbie to remove my top. It was then that her little voice piped up: "It's OK, Mommy. I won't laugh."

So much for thinking that I had kept my insecurities to myself. I was wrong.

Actress Angelina Jolie is one of the most recognizable and photographed women in the world. She appears in movies, magazines, and tabloid publications on a regular basis. Angelina's face, body, and weight undergo constant scrutiny by anyone and everyone who feels the need to chime into the discussion. So, what does this famous woman think of all of the attention paid to her appearance? Does the fact that our culture considers her beautiful have any impact on her personal opinion of herself?

Here are some quotes that I found online from Angelina:

> I don't see myself as beautiful, because I can see a lot of flaws. People have really odd opinions. They tell me I'm skinny, as if that's supposed to make me happy.[1]

> I'm odd looking. Sometimes I think I look like a funny muppet.[2]

> I struggle with low self-esteem all the time. I think everyone does. I have so much wrong with me, it's unbelievable.[3]

These quotes are not chronological, and I don't know in what context they were spoken. Even Angelina can have a few bad days. However, I think they demonstrate that even a woman plastered all over dozens of national and international magazine covers can think and feel the very same things that you do.

What fascinates me about women is that we would never criticize our friends the way that we harangue ourselves. Imagine the following dialogue:

> "Hi Jessica."
>
> "Hello, Emily. How are you today?"
>
> "I'm fine. But, honey, do you realize that your legs look like sausage rolls stuffed in those jeans? Oh, and that muffin top? Girl, you look like a breakfast combination from Jimmy Dean."

That conversation would never happen between friends. (If it does, you may want to rethink that friendship.) Yet we engage in that kind of dialogue with ourselves every time we look into the mirror. It's that "ME versus ME" battle again. Unfortunately, our mirrors have become an accessory to our campaign of self-condemnation and self-doubt.

We must understand what happens when we allow our feelings about our physical flaws to undermine our true value. We'll see how dangerous and hurtful it is for us to believe the ugly lie that we cannot be beautiful.

One of the reasons I share my stories is to give you permission to drag your stories and your beauty narratives out into the open so that you can stop struggling alone.

When I was a kid, my cousins called me "Buckteeth." I didn't get mad at them. It was true. I had buckteeth. However, when it turned into a nickname, I began to hate my teeth. Whenever I looked into the mirror, the first thing I saw each morning were those two large front teeth with a gap in between.

For a long time, I tried to smile without showing my teeth whenever a photo was taken. Whenever I looked at a picture, it seemed the only thing in the photo were my imperfect, large, gapped front teeth. Being so self-conscious of my teeth ruined many photographic memories for me.

Years have passed, but I'm still working through this issue. I don't really have buckteeth anymore because I've grown up enough that my large teeth fit my face. The gap remains, and I still struggle with whether I should fix the gap as the dentist suggests or I should overcome my insecurity and learn to accept my teeth as they are.

The entire situation bums me out because I love to smile. Furthermore, I have so much to smile about, so I couldn't stop smiling if I tried. Jesus has been so good and so faithful in my life that I would feel hypocritical if I didn't smile. I've discovered that when I smile, often people ask me why I have such a big smile, and that's my opening to share about God's goodness in my life. My smile is my cue to talk about Jesus.

Yes, I get the irony. That the very teeth I struggle with belong in a mouth that has been blessed by God to share a message with other women struggling with issues related to beauty. Crazy, right?

It's your turn. Rate how you feel about the following areas of your body:

	Love it!	Like it	It's okay	Struggle	Avoid thinking about
Hair	O	O	O	O	O
Eyes	O	O	O	O	O
Lips	O	O	O	O	O
Skin	O	O	O	O	O
Arms	O	O	O	O	O
Mid-section	O	O	O	O	O
Breasts	O	O	O	O	O
Hips	O	O	O	O	O
Legs	O	O	O	O	O
Feet	O	O	O	O	O

In my *Created with Curves* survey, I asked five hundred women to report their opinions about their various body parts using the same method as above. Even though I had a pretty good idea of how women would rate themselves, the actual data was quite enlightening. I noticed that 20 percent of survey participants skipped this question. Some women might have been too busy to finish the survey that day, but I think that the majority didn't feel comfortable answering.[4]

Here are the results:

	Love it!	Like it	It's okay	Struggle	Avoid thinking about
Hair	23.35% 99	37.03% 157	25% 106	12.03% 51	2.59% 11
Eyes	40.80% 173	39.62% 168	16.51% 70	2.59% 11	0.47% 2
Lips	19.76% 84	43.06% 183	32.24% 137	4% 17	0.94% 4
Skin	9.41% 40	28.00% 119	40% 170	19.53% 83	3.06% 13
Arms	5.92% 25	16.35% 69	33.89% 143	29.62% 125	14.22% 60
Mid-section	2.59% 11	5.66% 24	16.51% 70	38.68% 164	36.56% 155
Breasts	8.71% 37	23.06% 98	34.59% 147	20.71% 88	12.94% 55
Hips	5.42% 23	13.21% 56	33.02% 140	25.24% 107	23.11% 98
Legs	7.31% 31	18.16% 77	26.18% 111	26.18% 111	22.17% 94
Feet	8.75% 37	26.48% 112	37.59% 159	12.77% 54	14.42% 61

When it comes to what we love about our bodies, the "eyes" have it! Over 40 percent of women love their eyes. A healthy number of us love our lips, too.

What do we hate? Not surprising, the survey results reveal a scant 2.5 percent of women love their midsections, and only 5 percent of women love their hips, with the majority of women stating that these areas are a struggle or they avoid thinking about this area of their body.

Rating ourselves is about more than just the isolated parts. When we look in the mirror and don't like what we see, what are we saying to ourselves as a result? How are we judging ourselves? How are we judging our abilities? Our self-worth? Our hopes and dreams?

FLAW FINDING

Next, I asked the ladies the following open-ended question in the survey: "When you look into the mirror, what are some of the words you've used to describe yourself?" I'm going to start with the women who looked in the mirror and shared positive feedback about themselves:

> "A gem for life"
> "Gorgeous and blessed! Voluptuous! Precious as rubies.
> Woman of color"
> "I'm beautiful, amazing, lovely, God-fearing, blessed, over-
> comer, and a role-model"
> "Strong and independent"
> "I'm beautiful, confident, and radiant"
> "Strong, athletic, driven"
> "Kind, loving, compassionate"
> "Unique, unconventional, beautiful"[5]

Be honest, how do you feel about the responses you just read? We love it when a woman feels good about herself, but secretly, we really want that woman to be us!

Let's review another set of responses that women gave:

"Ordinary, plain, nothing special"
"Fat. Ugly. Undesirable."
"Gross. Why. Ehh, its OK. Fat. Ugly."
"Flabby, dorky, let myself go"
"Overweight, need to work on my abs"
"Hideous, disgrace, waste"
"Ugh! Fat, scared, broken"
"FAT! Wrinkling, ugly, FAT!"[6]

Another surprising finding was that the number one word women used to describe themselves was *fat*. When that word popped up in the survey analytics, I wanted to cry. Of all the words we could use to describe ourselves, why did so many women use the word *fat*? Not everyone did, but a full quarter of the women surveyed used that word. Furthermore, only 6.7 percent of women used the word *beautiful*.

My little survey captured so many different stories of struggle. Here is another story:

> When I was about 16, the boy I liked told me that my eye-lids had too many veins on them. Since that day I have worn concealer on my eyelids to hide the veins. I am now married and asked my husband about a year into our marriage, (I had decided to not wear concealer one day) if the veins were bothering him. He looked at me like I was completely insane, and I only wear it now when I am feeling very insecure. . . . I feel silly about having worn the concealer for 16 years![7]

BEING ON GUARD DUTY

We've already talked about how we are engaged in an ugly struggle with beauty. Although Satan is working to discourage us from seeing our God-given beauty, he's not the only one trying to steal our victory. We're doing a pretty good job of self-sabotage, too. We need to do a better job of protecting ourselves on the field of battle.

The ugly struggle with beauty is a relentless war that starts in the mirror each morning and lasts all day. Our hearts are attacked by hurtful words, painful insecurity, and so much more. Perhaps, we should locate some guards for our hearts. Listen to these words: "Guard your heart above all else, for it determines the course of your life" (Proverbs 4:23).

During conflict or war, each side posts guards to protect and defend their battle resources. It would be crazy to just leave weapons and ammunition out in the open for the enemy to attack and steal. Protection is proactive.

Our hearts need to be protected. Our hearts are more than just a beating organ. The heart is the center of your emotions, intelligence, and soul. Think about all of the disparaging words that you've used to describe yourself in the mirror: fat, wrinkly, plain, curvy, dorky. All of these words impact our hearts in some way. The cumulative effect of those words will impact how we manage our interactions with others as well as how we handle ourselves in the world.

What are some of the ways we can guard our hearts while we engage in our ugly struggle with beauty? In future chapters we're going to talk about being on the offensive and developing our beauty, but now, we need to protect ourselves while we mobilize to fight. There are lots of practical tips in future chapters, but the first step is in recognizing that the enemy is out there and waiting to strike. So, how do we guard our hearts?

Think of a security system in a home. Sensors are strategically placed around the home in areas a thief might try to breach, such as windows or doorways. Even though the homeowner needs to have doors and windows, those openings are less secure than the home's walls. The sensors placed over those vulnerable areas are the first line of defense. If someone tries to gain access without permission, the sensor sounds an alarm.

You and I need sensors. We need to know the places where we are most vulnerable when it comes to our ugly struggle with beauty. I'm vulnerable whenever I think about my teeth or see someone who looks like me with perfect teeth. Another vulnerable area is the department store dressing room. The fluorescent lighting and gigantic mirror intimidate me, especially when I am not feeling my best. I'm very vulnerable in that moment.

Where or when are you most vulnerable? Perhaps it's when you visit your mom and she reminds you how much skinnier you were in high school. Maybe you feel vulnerable when you are out with your girlfriends and everyone has a boyfriend or husband except for you. When do you feel most vulnerable? These are the places where you need sensors.

The goal isn't just to identify but to protect. Our journey toward winning our ugly struggle with beauty includes a specific strategy for victory that will begin with understanding God's design for beauty.

We've gotten through several chapters on our journey together. If you haven't done so, I encourage you to share your journey with a friend. It can be overwhelming and discouraging to unearth painful beauty narratives or wallow in our flaws alone. It might take courage, but invite another woman along on this journey with you. Read a chapter a week and talk through the questions. While it might be awkward at first, you'll appreciate having someone to talk with during this important period of your life.

BEAUTY MARK

Overfocusing on our flaws leads to undervaluing our self-worth.

GROUP DISCUSSION QUESTIONS

1. What did your mother or other influential female in your life used to say about her body? Did her opinion of herself have an effect on you?

2. Does it seem strange to you that Angelina Jolie and other female celebrities would have angst about their physical features? Do you think they genuinely feel that way or not?

3. Discuss the Created with Curves results. What surprised you about the data? What didn't surprise you? How did you rate yourself?

4. Why do so few women rate themselves highly for abs or thighs?

5. In the last section, Barb talked about the importance of understanding our vulnerabilities in our ugly struggle with beauty. Where are some places that women are vulnerable?

6. Can you think of a woman who spends a lot of time flaw finding? What does Proverbs 4:23 tell you about the probable direction of her ugly struggle with beauty? Is there any way you might be able to help her?

PERSONAL JOURNALING QUESTIONS

1. List the areas of your body that you love and the areas that you don't like or even hate. Which list is longer? How do you feel about that?

2. When you look into the mirror, what are some of the words you use to describe yourself?

3. Currently, what is the state of your heart? Are you protecting it from the thoughts or people that can cause your heart harm? If so, how are you protecting it? If not, what do you think you need to do differently?

BEAUTY'S GOODNESS

Then God looked over all he had made,
and he saw that it was very good!
—*Genesis 1:31*

Let's step back for a few moments from examining the topic of beauty as it relates to us and look at beauty in the context of the world around us. Can we agree that God created a beautiful world around us?

If God didn't care about physical beauty, then why did He create sunrises that take our breath away? Why did He create fluffy white clouds and blue skies that inspire us to cut out of work early on summer days? If physical beauty was irrelevant or superfluous, then why do we plant flowering plants or give flowers for important occasions? Home Depot, Lowes, and every local florist and greenhouse is in business because God decided to share His beautiful nature with our world.

For me, one of the most beautiful places in the world is located thirty minutes outside of La Ceiba, Honduras, at a beautiful resort called the Palma Real Hotel. This glorious resort is nestled between the lush, green, majestic Cordillera Nombre de Dios mountain range and the white sand and foamy blue waters of the Caribbean.

When I visit the Hotel Palma, I stake out a spot in the sand where the foamy ocean water crashes against the sandy shore. I love sitting in the sand at the water's edge and feeling the remnants of each wave stroke over my toes. Each time I scan across the distant waterline of the vast Caribbean Ocean and as I gaze out on endless blue water, the words of Psalm 19:1 float across my mind: "The heavens declare the glory of God, the skies proclaim the work of his hands" (NIV).

Resting in the sand while sitting on that coast is where I see, feel, and touch the workmanship of God's beautiful character.

Closer to home, there is a park near my house where I love to sit on a weathered bench under the towering trees high above the river's edge. When I sit on one of those benches underneath the vast sky, I am again reminded of God's nature and character. Likewise, I am convinced that God not only admires physical beauty but also wants to intentionally share it with us so that we can know that aspect of His character.

For me, the presence of pure beauty always reflects the presence of God. And when we recognize this truth, we must also embrace the following: BEAUTY IS GOD'S CREATION, NOT OURS.

Although we may struggle with our individual relationships with beauty, our Creator God shows us the importance of physical beauty. The evidence of this beauty is all around for us to see, to enjoy, and most of all, to thank God for providing for our usage and our enjoyment.

Where's your favorite place in the world? Isn't it amazing how your body just seems to know you are getting close to that beautiful, relaxing, or inspiring place? Perhaps it's a cottage on the lake. Maybe it's a campsite nestled in the mountains or a sandy beach that stretches for miles.

In June 1999, my husband and I visited Victoria Falls, Zimbabwe. We flew across the Atlantic and over the vast expanse of the Africa dessert before landing thirty hours later on a dirt airstrip in remote Zimbabwe.

The only thing I knew about waterfalls was what I knew about Niagara Falls, which wasn't much. I was way more worried about running into giant African tarantulas than I was excited about seeing Victoria Falls. Seeing any kind of tarantula would usually be a deal breaker; however, after flying thirty hours overseas, I strapped on my courage and got into our open-air vehicles for a long drive to one of the most beautiful places in the world.

Early the next morning, my heart swelled as we stood on the banks of Zambezi River that feeds into the "falls that roar" in the cold wind and gazed out at the peaceful and serene landscape. Curious hippos would bob to the surface from time to time as we walked along the water's edge. I tried to picture the hand of God setting the trees, plants, and animals into place.

On our nine-day trip, there were several times when I had the sensation that we were gazing out on distant landscapes that had only been touched by the hand of God, never humans. Although I can't say that for sure, there were times when the purity of the beauty around us made me think so. Except for the day when my canoe ran aground and remained stuck about twenty feet from a sleeping crocodile. That was not my favorite day.

There was a God-moment that summed up the trip for me. It was the last day, and we were touring the actual Victoria Falls. The spray from the waterfall created a persistent fine mist that poured off our rain jackets. As we walked toward the end of the waterfall, I saw the top of a rainbow come into view. As we got closer and the full rainbow came into view, my eyes filled with tears before I even realized what was going on. My body sensed the evidence of God's beauty before my brain. Then, I had this thought: *Here is a place on the planet, not made by human hands, that has displayed perpetual evidence of God's promise ever since the waterfall came into existence.*

There is something that God wants us to know about Him when we look at the beauty of His creation, mainly, that He is the Creator of beauty, not us. We must take our cues and attitude about beauty from God's viewpoint and not our own.

CREATOR AND CAREGIVER

I am a horticultural grim reaper. My mother-in-law insists that there's hope for me. But there's a pitiful-looking rhododendron in my backyard that says "not a chance." This is sad considering that I just love flowers. Every spring, I stroll through my historical neighborhood inhaling the deep perfume smell of lilacs, lavender, hydrangeas, and more. Their colors and their fragrances speak to a place deep within my soul.

Lately, I've been watching the leaves on the tall, sturdy trees in my neighborhood turn from dark green to deep red, bright orange, and lemonade yellow. As much as I love the rich green color of summer, I just love it when those fall colors begin streaking their beautiful hue. Who tells them to do that each year?

Matthew 6 is one of my favorite chapters in the Bible. Jesus is teaching a lot of *do*s and *don't*s about life to the crowd. Starting in verse 26, Jesus tells the crowd not to worry, and he uses God's creation as an example:

> Look at the birds. They don't plant or harvest or store food in barns, for your heavenly Father feeds them. And aren't you far more valuable to him than they are? Can all your worries add a single moment to your life? And why worry about your clothing? Look at the lilies of the field and how they grow. They don't work or make their clothing, yet Solomon in all his glory was not dressed as beautifully as they are. And if God cares so wonderfully for wildflowers that are here today and thrown into the fire tomorrow, he will certainly care for you. Why do you have so little faith? (vv. 26-30)

Have you ever held a fine, white lily in your hand? Those flowers are fragile and don't last for more than a few weeks, yet God used His exquisite, creative eye to design something so beautiful just for us to enjoy. In this passage, Jesus reminds us that just as God has poured care and attention on the created world around us, we have substantially more value in God's eyes. Even though flowers may be temporary, their beauty still has value, yet not as much value as we have.

When I look at the flowers, especially the multitude of varieties, I smile. The array of colors and designs seems endless, and the fragrances of those flowers are the basis for many of the finest perfumes we wear today. All of this points to the idea that God is intentional about physical beauty.

THE BEAUTY OF A ROSE

Have you ever thought of why only women are named after flowers? Guys generally aren't named after flowers. The closest thing I think a guy could be named would be Bud. Floral-themed names, such as Rose, Lily, Magnolia, or Amethyst, are generally reserved for women. What is the relationship between flowers and women? Could this relationship provide some insight into how God sees each of us as women? (By the way, my grandmother's name was Magnolia. She was one of the most magnificent people I've ever known. I'll tell you more about her later.)

Last February, I attended the funeral of a lovely woman named Rose Stewart. Her daughter-in-law, Jera, is one of my dearest friends and was Mrs. Stewart's caregiver during the early stages of dementia.

While Alzheimer's might have stolen Mrs. Stewart's memories, hundreds of people remembered the tremendous impact she had on their lives. Mrs. Stewart never became famous or drew large crowds. She was a housewife who raised five children and lived with her husband, Ralph, until he passed away. At her funeral, while gazing at dozens of red roses on her casket and listening to many people testifying to her life, I realized that this soft-spoken woman's legacy had beauty written all over it.

Here is the poem that one of her sons, Bill, wrote as a tribute to his mother, Mrs. Rose Stewart:

No matter where you plant its seed, the truth is I
suppose,
Despite life's many obstacles, a Rose will be a rose.
Among the weeds and rocky soil, it somehow pushes
through,
And with it, it brings warmth and joy, 'cause that's what
Roses do.
Admired for its beauty, and protected by its thorns,
Influencing the landscape of the garden it adorns.
Displaying vibrant colors with a fragrance oh so fine,
The Rose affects other plants, and makes them want to
shine.
No ego, and no false pretense above the other flowers,
Restoring frayed relationships while extolling God's
great power,
The Rose fulfills its purpose, though its life is one brief
season,
Obeying the "Great Gardener's" plan and trusting in
His reasons.[1]

BEAUTY MARK
It's okay to appreciate physical beauty. God does.

GROUP DISCUSSION QUESTIONS

1. Where's the most beautiful place you've ever visited? How did you feel when you were there?

2. *The main idea of this chapter is that GOD IS THE CRE-ATOR OF BEAUTY, NOT US. What does the presence of natural beauty (flowers, trees, mountains, and so on) reveal to you about God?*

3. *How does the regenerating beauty of plants and flowers encourage us in a world that contains many ugly things?*

4. *Did you have any new insights about how God created our bodies to be expressions of His beauty?*

5. *There are a variety of verses about the beauty of God's creation. Which one of the verses left the biggest impression on you? Why?*

PERSONAL JOURNALING QUESTIONS

1. *Where is a place that you'd love to visit one day? Why would you like to travel there?*

2. *Where is the most beautiful place you've ever been? Why is that location beautiful to you?*

3. *When you think about how God took the time and attention to create a beautiful world for us to enjoy, what does that say to you about the time and attention He put into creating you?*

DEFINING "DIVINE BEAUTY"

For the Scriptures say, "You must be holy because I am holy."
—*1 Peter 1:16*

Beauty is in the eye of the beholder
and it may be necessary from time to time to give
a stupid or misinformed beholder a black eye.
—*Miss Piggy, The Muppets*[1]

A few times a year, I pilgrimage an hour north to IKEA with a few girlfriends. Even though an hour's drive isn't very far, it's far enough for the trip to be special each time we go. Our purpose for going to IKEA is simple. We want to *ooh* and *ahhh* and find lots of pretty things.

IKEA houses three floors stuffed with thousands of *ooh* and *ahh* moments. The girls and I love mentally redecorating the different rooms of our homes as we weave in and out of different displays and vignettes. As we walk and talk, the girls and I judge the merchandise according to what we find pleasing or displeasing to look at.

One of us might point to a set of bookcases, curtains, or patterned textile and exclaim, "Oh, don't you just love how this looks!" Sometimes, we'll agree with her. Sometimes, we won't. We don't have any rules regarding what we love and what we don't; it's a matter of personal preference.

Doesn't it seem like defining beauty is often a matter of personal preference?

I shared the dictionary definition of *beauty* in the first chapter, but it really doesn't give us an objective picture or boundaries. For a few chapters, we talked about where to find beauty and its impact, but now, we are back to trying to define beauty. It's a difficult task. Perhaps, this is why philosophers finally waved the white flag and let individuals or cultures decide what constitutes beauty. But what happens when we have differing interpretations or applications of the definition? Can something be beautiful if one person says it is but another person says it isn't? If that is the case, then where does that leave us as humans? Does our beauty rely on the opinions or perception of others or of ourselves?

Many people (maybe even you) think that beauty is a shallow topic and unworthy of our study or best thinking. Yet I believe that beauty is a spiritual matter because, as women, beauty affects our hearts, minds, and our souls, and these are places that are under God's domain. So yes, beauty is a spiritual matter and worthy of the time and effort you put into figuring this out.

There were more than four hundred definitions of beauty submitted by more than five hundred *Created with Curves* survey participants. How could something that is supposedly defined have so many different interpretations?

Here are a few responses:

"You have to have a beautiful heart to have complete beauty."
"Being comfortable in your own skin."
"Beauty is when you feel good about how you look."

"What is on the inside, not on the outside."

"Friendly, loving, nice, kind, gracious, and hospitable."

"Not me."[2]

As expected, most definitions included words such as *loving, kind*, and *confident*. Some of the physical characteristics included words like *healthy, fit*, and *proportionate features*. I appreciated one participant who added that *cleanliness* should be a part of the definition of beauty. Amen, sister.

In our culture, there is no absolute definition of beauty. Scientists have tried to apply objective constructs to measure beauty. They've measured for proportionality, symmetry, or harmony, but to no avail. Our best human thinking is caught up in a black hole that just absorbs our inputs and opinions but never reveals a true answer.

This is why beauty frustrates us. Our best definition of beauty is subjective or left up to our individual opinions. It appears that anything or anyone really can be beautiful until someone comes around and declares otherwise. Others have used beauty as a weapon to crush or destroy women. How many girls have rejected being identified as females by binding their breasts or shaving their heads? What inner or outer tragedy robbed them of the truth about beauty?

My friends, we are caught in a horrible swirling vortex of opinion without a clear direction. In the whirlwind, opinions from media, advertisers, family, and friends strike at our hearts and minds with no protection or filter. Too many of us are suffering as a result.

This is why I believe that the phrase *Beauty is in the eye of the beholder* is the most dangerous phrase a woman could ever believe.[3] It is a lie. These words are supposed to bring some sort of freedom to proclaim beauty in anyone or anything. Unfortunately, the perception of beauty can be created or destroyed by anyone and everyone who weighs in with an opinion.

Why do we have so many different kinds of definitions? Should we just give up and allow beauty to be defined in any way that we want to define it?

I will tell you this: if you understand who God is, then you will understand beauty.

DIVINE BEAUTY

When we speak of beauty, its origins, or even its meaning, the nature of God anchors our discussion. Any attempt to explain beauty must stem from God's divine character and nothing else. This is why we call the highest form of beauty, divine beauty.

Although God cannot be explained or defined in human terms, He shows us His character and nature in the Scriptures. Why? God wants us to know Him. In his book *The Holiness of God*, R. C. Sproul identifies three qualities of God's character that define His holiness. These qualities also provide a framework that we can use to pattern our personal definitions of beauty:

God is TRUTH.
God is GOOD.
God is BEAUTIFUL.[6]

Depending on your spiritual journey or your worldview, those three statements about God will resonate with you in different ways. One of the struggles present in our culture is the struggle to accept absolutes. It's considered polite to adopt an anything-goes mentality to life. We hesitate to apply a right-or-wrong value to any standard because we fear being labeled as intolerant, prejudiced, or ignorant.

Yet God is absolute. He is not relative to anything else in our world. Even if your view of God is filled with questions or if you believe that there are many ways to reach heaven, chances are you would agree that

God has no equal. So this would mean that whatever qualities we ascribe to God, no one or nothing is going to be a better example or version of that quality. Furthermore, God would be the ultimate of such a quality.

Therefore . . .

- Since God is TRUTH, then God cannot lie or undermine Himself. Therefore, what He declares as truth is absolute and cannot be undermined or discredited as not true.
- Since God is GOOD, then He is void of anything that is not good, and everything that is good has its origins in God.
- Since God is BEAUTIFUL, He has no ugliness or distortion, and His beauty transcends our hearts and minds and soaks into our souls.[7]

Each of these qualities is a part of God's nature, and together, these qualities paint a picture of God, and this is the picture of divine beauty.

Definition of divine beauty: The true, good, and beautiful nature of God.

THE BEAUTY OF HOLINESS

There's a word that describes the special kind of uniqueness of God: holy. The ancient meaning of *holy* is "set apart."[4]

God is holy or set apart because His nature is the ultimate and unmatched in truth, goodness, and beauty. His nature provides a new (or different) measuring stick for those who are used to measuring their lives by our culture's standards of truth, goodness, and beauty.

However, using the word *holiness* in our culture tends to spark accusations of intolerance, prejudice, or extremism. This is unfortunate because the essence of holiness is being in a class by itself.

Could it be that when we establish an eternal connection with God and we embrace our standing as being created in His image, that we realize that we are beautiful? Not because of anything that we've done, but only because we are made in the image of a beautiful God.

The well-known movie *Mean Girls*[5] provides a picture of how our culture can manipulate the idea of "set apart." No one is going to argue that the Plastics clique was "holy," but queen bee Regina and crew made it clear that they were a cut above the rest of the school. The Plastics used their beauty to create a divide between them and others in order to dominate and intimidate.

Being made in the image of God doesn't make us gods. Repeat, being created in the image of God does not make us gods. There is only one God, and it is not us.

Still, being created in God's image means that we should never look in the mirror and believe anything said about us that is not consistent with God's character.

Furthermore, God invites us to connect with Him and share in His holy nature by walking in His truth, goodness, and beauty.

If God is holy or "set apart" because of His perfect nature, should we also pursue that same holiness? Yes. Why should we? Because God calls us to: "So you must live as God's obedient children. Don't slip back into your old ways of living to satisfy your own desires. You didn't know any better then. But now you must be holy in everything you do, just as God who chose you is holy. For the Scriptures say, 'You must be holy because I am holy'" (1 Peter 1:14-16).

In the early centuries, the Apostle Peter was addressing a new audience of believers who lived in a culture that valued appearances and self-satisfaction. Instead, believers, including us, are called to focus on God rather than self. Of course, living for God will set us apart from our culture.

CONFORM VERSUS TRANSFORM

I attended a mid-sized, suburban high school with about four hundred students in my graduating class. At that time, I considered myself "preppie," meaning that I wore my shirt collar standing up and my pants legs pegged tight. Both fashion statements were the classic sign of being preppie in the 1980s. In fact, most of the kids at my school were preppie, so I fit right in.

I love how Sproul defines *conforming* versus *transforming*. The word *conform* means "with structure." When we conform, we go along with what's going on. In our beauty culture, conforming happens when we take our attitudes and beliefs from the world around us regarding what we wear, how we should pose, or how to interpret what we see in the mirror. When we conform, we chase the ideas of an elusive beauty that we all want to catch and claim. Even if we are not trying, we are secretly envious of the ones who are trying. Maybe we aren't trying because we don't think we can do it, so we're lamenting the fact that we'll never be *that* kind of beauty.

However, when we infuse the pursuit of holiness into our life, our focus shifts from going with the crowd toward a new direction. The Apostle Paul explains it in Romans 12:2: "Don't copy the behavior and customs of this world, but let God transform you into a new person by changing the way you think. Then you will learn to know God's will for you, which is good and pleasing and perfect."

Our world wants us to believe its beauty standard. Frankly, advertisers, media, and beauty companies have done a great job in pressuring us to conform to their beauty standards. However, God wants to take us beyond what the world is trying to offer and elevate our lives and our purpose.

Transform means to "go across structure" or "beyond structure." When we are transformed, we are set apart, and we recognize that we are set apart for God's purpose, which is to make us more like Him.

Therefore, if we become more like God, then we will reflect His holy nature. Following this progression, the more we reflect God's nature, the more we radiate His beauty.

Not only that, but we also become more righteous. Notice I did not say that we become more *religious*. Lucky for us, Jesus wasn't a religious guy. In a confrontation with religious leaders, Jesus condemns their false attempts at holiness and righteousness. These men believed that their outward acts could cover for the cesspools that festered in their hearts, and Jesus called them on it in Matthew 23:27-28: "What sorrow awaits you teachers of religious law and you Pharisees. Hypocrites! For you are like whitewashed tombs—beautiful on the outside but filled on the inside with dead people's bones and all sorts of impurity. Outwardly you look like righteous people, but inwardly your hearts are filled with hypocrisy and lawlessness."

Jesus hated the idea that people avoided dealing with their heart issues and assumed that putting on a show would be sufficient enough. Not in God's eyes. He cares too much for you to bemoan or obsess about the façade without allowing Him to transform your heart.

Divine beauty is a standard that does not change. When we allow God to transform us at the deepest levels of our existence, we will understand the true, good, and beautiful nature of God.

BEAUTY MARK
Divine beauty is the true, good, and beautiful nature of God.

GROUP DISCUSSION QUESTIONS

1. What is your definition of beauty? Why is beauty so hard to define?

2. What is the definition of divine beauty? Does this make sense to you?

3. Most women know that what is on the inside matters most, but too many women still don't have a benchmark for figuring out which qualities or characteristics should be the most important. How do you feel about this definition of divine beauty?

4. How is the concept of holiness connected to our discussion about beauty?

5. Read Romans 12:2. What are some of the ways our culture tries to get us to conform to its standard of beauty?

6. What were two things that you discovered in this chapter that you hadn't really thought about before? Has this discovery prompted you to consider thinking or behaving differently? If so, in which ways?

PERSONAL JOURNALING QUESTIONS

1. How have you been tempted or struggle with our culture's beauty standards? If you have managed this tension successfully, how have you done it?

2. How are you doing at being "holy" or "set apart" for God's service? Have you identified places in your life where you are still too tied to the culture and should be tied closer to God?

3. Read Galatians 5:22-23. How are you doing with the Fruit of the Spirit? Which areas has God been working in your life? Which areas do you need to give Him more room to work?

SEE GOD FIRST

*Seek the Kingdom of God above all else, and live righteously,
and he will give you everything you need.*
—Matthew 6:33

Lizzie Velasquez was once labeled the "world's ugliest woman."[1] She was born with an extremely rare condition that prevents her from keeping or storing body fat. She weighs only sixty pounds, and even though she is in her twenties, her skin hangs loose in many areas. Lizzie is also blind in one eye and has limited vision in the other. According to Lizzie's website, there are only three other people in the world with a condition similar to hers.

One day, high-school-aged Lizzie was clicking through YouTube looking for some music. As Lizzie scanned through the column of related videos, she saw a video with a photo that looked really familiar. Imagine Lizzie's surprise when she realized that she was the subject of a YouTube video. Lizzie explains what happened next: "There is an eight-second video with no sound that over four million people saw of only me—calling me the 'world's ugliest woman.' I literally felt like someone was putting their hand through the computer and punching me over and over again."

Then, Lizzie made a decision that she would call a "defining moment" in her life. She decided to read through every single comment. And every single comment was negative. Many of the comments suggested that Lizzie walk around with a bag over her head or even kill herself. Here is how Lizzie explains her feelings about finding out that based on a photo that was taken when she was eleven years old, that she was now defined online as the "world's ugliest woman":

> My confidence level went from being up here to way down here to non-existent. In an instant it was brought down completely. I wanted to make them feel bad for hiding behind their computer screen and make them feel bad. What am I going to accomplish? I am going to be fighting a never ending battle that will never prove anything? But something clicked in me. A little voice that I knew was God. "Just wait. Let it go and wait."

By leaning on her faith, her friends, and her family, Lizzie made the decision to keep living and pursuing her goals and dreams. Rather than fight back, Lizzie moved forward and trusted God. Lizzie has graduated from college and is the author of the book *Be Beautiful, Be You.* As a motivational speaker, Lizzie sees that how God created her is in accordance with His perfect plan:

> My relationship with God is better than ever. When I realized that I wanted to be a speaker, I said, "God, I get you now. I get it. I still have some questions, but I get it. You made me the girl that I am for a reason. You gave me all those struggles growing up to make me strong. You made me different so that I could see the beauty that isn't defined by the media. And yes, I am still learning but the feeling that I get because I know that God is working through me and helping me tell you something is the greatest feeling in the entire world."

I love Lizzie's story. She reminds us of how God truly sees us: as manifestations of His marvelous, perfect workmanship! When God sees us—more specifically, when God sees you—He is not looking at your thighs, He is not looking at your perfect eyebrows, and He doesn't care if you've got that coveted gap between your knees.

God wants us to shine as beacons on a hill, specially designed to radiate His truth and beauty to women in our world who are desperate to find a beauty that is pure and true.

Yet, my friends, our God-given beauty cannot shine if we are covering it up behind bad attitudes or beliefs about ourselves. Our God-given beauty cannot shine through if we carry ourselves as if we are an afterthought instead of as the physical bodies that God specially designed for each of us.

REFRAMING WHAT WE SEE

I watch my 12-year-old daughter look at herself in the mirror the way that I look at myself. I am careful not to criticize myself in front of her so that she does not do that to herself. She is beautiful and inspires me to work on my own self-esteem concerning beauty.
—Created with Curves *participant*[2]

What do you focus on when you look in the mirror? Are you looking for wrinkles or checking to see if any roots are showing through? Do you avoid the mirror altogether?

Every morning, I stumble into the bathroom to start my day. My first task of each day is to conduct what I like to call my "101-point inspection" on my face and body. Starting up top, I survey the landscape of my face, hair, and neck to see if any new lines, spots, wrinkles, or unwanted hair have appeared in places where they should not be. Then, I turn sideways in the mirror to check whether my midsection looks thicker or thinner than the day before. I zero in on my lower stomach area because if something went wrong overnight, it's going to appear there first. Next, I'll swing my hips around to see if my rear end has lowered any more since the day before. I admit there is no objective way to know for sure, but I check anyway.

The final phase of the inspection is the weigh-in. Although many women avoid the scale, I invite this misery by stepping on the scale at least two or three times a week. There are rules to the weigh-in to make sure the weight is the lowest possible. I believe that my most successful weigh-ins happen first thing in the morning, after I've used the restroom and, most important, when I am naked as a jaybird.

Whether you are a supermodel or you consider yourself a frump, what you see in the mirror matters. I'm not trying to make a value statement of whether or not you should care about what you see; I'm just stating a fact. What you see isn't the most important thing about you, but *how* you see yourself does matter. Our interpretation of our reflection is inextricably linked to our emotions. When we feel good about what we see in the mirror, it has a positive impact on how we feel. Conversely, when we don't like what we see in the mirror, that also has an impact on how we feel.

So, this isn't just about bemoaning your midsection or loathing your thighs. It's about the words you use to describe yourself: ugly, fat, lazy, ashamed, depressed, sad, hopeless. We say those things to ourselves enough and we believe them. Once we believe them, it takes a lot to "un-believe" them, especially if we repeat those words to ourselves day after day.

What have you been saying to yourself in the mirror lately? Honey, listen to me: if God were standing next to you when you were looking in the mirror, how would your conversation in the mirror change? *(Ouch!)*

SEE GOD FIRST

I want to introduce you to Matthew 6:33. Jesus teaches on a variety of topics in this chapter. One of those topics is worry. Jesus knew that when we worry about something, that worry shifts our focus away from where God wants it to be. Therefore, Jesus challenges us to redirect our thoughts in Matthew 6:33: "Seek the Kingdom of God above all else, and live righteously, and he will give you everything you need."

The first part of the verse is summed up like this: see God first.

What does it mean to "see God first"? The original Greek word for *seek* is *zeteo*. Seeking is serious business! It's more than just looking, like looking for one's keys or an outfit to wear to work. In this case, "seeking" is a high-stakes pursuit of searching, the kind of searching that a parent does when his or her child wanders off in the store. That's the kind of seeking that God wants us to do. We're not called just to look for a casual connection with God. Rather, we're called to devote our effort and energy to connecting with Him. At its essence, *zeteo* is an intense seeking with desire and purpose; therefore, *seek* means to desire or crave.[3]

I love cheesecake. Its creamy goodness just makes me happy. The best place to eat cheesecake is at The Cheesecake Factory. I heart their Reese's Peanut Butter Chocolate Cake Cheesecake. So, a few times a year, I seek out that cheesecake. And a gym. Even if it takes an hour to get a table, I'll wait just so that I can enjoy my meal and get that cheesecake.

Do I desire God that much? I hope so. If I am going to claim victory over my ugly struggle with beauty, I must seek God first. When I seek God first, this means that I subject my opinions and beliefs about my body through the filter of God's truth. Too often, I allow my beliefs and life's experiences to overwhelm God's truth. That won't lead to victory.

When we see God first, that means we have to take our eyes off ourselves, our history, and our imperfections or shortcomings and put our eyes on God. Our reward is that we experience the joy that comes from seeing God's goodness, blessing, and purpose for the heart, mind, and body that He has given to us.

YOU ARE ENOUGH ALREADY
BECAUSE GOD SAYS SO!

Our greatest fear is that we are not enough already. So, each morning we look for whatever we can find in the mirror to validate our fear. Unfortunately, we consume endless cultural messages about what kinds of flaws we should be looking for.

Yet, here is what one scriptural writer says about how God sees you and me in Psalm 139:13-14: "You made all the delicate, inner parts of my body and knit me together in my mother's womb. Thank you for making me so wonderfully complex! Your workmanship is marvelous—how well I know it."

This classic Old Testament passage captures the truth about how much love and attention God used when creating each and every one of us. We must always see ourselves from God's perspective and allow His attitude toward us to become our attitude toward ourselves.

My sister, whether you believe this or not, God's eyes were on every single detail of your body. He shaped your eyes, your lips, the contours of your cheeks. He arranged the DNA of your body—including hair color, skin color, body shape, and height—according to his omnipotent plan.

Our Creator God does not make mistakes. Most of all, nothing can take away from your status as a created being in the image of God. You may have been neglected, abused, bullied, or forgotten, but your heart, mind, body, and soul still have the imprint of God.

PRACTICAL STEPS:
HOW DO WE SEE GOD FIRST?

How can we practice applying Matthew 6:33 to our lives when we stand in front of the mirror? Here are three things that we should see that remind us of God's truth about us and our purpose when we are tempted to focus on our physical flaws:

STEP ONE: SEE THE GOODNESS

Even though you may not like the size or shape of one of your body parts, focus on the idea that this feature was created for you by God. Remember, everything that God made fits His definition of goodness. We need to proclaim that goodness and adopt God's truth rather than our own. Say the following to yourself in the mirror:

> God, thank You for my body, crafted by Your all-powerful, creative hands. Genesis 1:31 says that You have made all things good, including me. I reject any thought or belief that contradicts the reality of Your marvelous workmanship of my physical being.

STEP TWO: SEE THE BLESSING

Just as Lizzie Velasquez realizes the blessing of her physical condition and how it allows God to use her in magnificent ways, we also have to see God's blessing in our bodies. Let's take a moment to express our gratitude for whatever feature of our body usually causes us to criticize or condemn ourselves. Say the following to yourself in the mirror. Repeat this sentence for every body part that is a struggle for you:

> God, you've blessed me with this body. God, I struggle with _____. Today, I'm going to honor this part of my body by remembering that You created it.

STEP THREE: SEE THE PURPOSE

Each part of our body has a God-defined purpose. We don't have to overthink this one, but we can easily condemn certain features of our body rather than give thanks. We are all unique creations, and God has a specific plan and purpose for our hearts, minds, bodies, and life experiences. Say the following to yourself in the mirror:

God, it is so easy for me to say mean things about my body in the mirror. Instead, I recognize that You have a plan and purpose for my life. This means that I must look at my physical body as a tool that You will use to make a difference in someone else's life.

Today, God, I will use:

My mouth to: _____.
My arms to: _____.
My legs to: _____.
My feet to: _____.

BEAUTY MARK
Seeking God first helps us reframe what we see in the mirror each day.

GROUP DISCUSSION QUESTIONS

1. Describe your morning grooming routine. Do you scan your face and body like Barb's "101-point inspection," or do you avoid the mirror?

2. What did you think of Lizzie Velasquez's story? (If you have computer access, take ten minutes and watch her You-Tube video titled "Bullied girl voted ugliest on the Internet gives an amazing speech.")

3. Matthew 6:33 tells us to seek God first above all else. Barb discusses this verse in the context of our discussion about beauty. What does it mean to you to see God first in the mirror? What kind of impact could that have on your life?

4. How can seeing God first reframe our perspective on our life's experiences?

PERSONAL JOURNALING QUESTIONS

1. If Jesus were standing next to you in front of the mirror, how much of your self-description would change? What words or phrases would you stop using to describe yourself?

2. How do you think Jesus would respond to your self-debasement in the mirror? What verses would he use? Would he be speaking to you out of love or condemnation?

3. Where are you at in your spiritual journey? Think about the definition of seek. Are you seeking God as defined by Matthew 6:33? What would it look like for you to seek after God above all else?

4. Is it time for you to surrender some words or phrases and never use them again to describe yourself?

WHAT HAVE I DONE
TO MYSELF?

How precious are your thoughts about me, O God.
They cannot be numbered!
—*Psalm 139:17*

In the previous chapter, I hope you were inspired and challenged to see God first whenever you look in the mirror or see yourself in a photograph. Just so you know, I'm working on it, too.

Yet, I have this nagging suspicion that some of you still struggle to see God first in the mirror. Deep inside, you believe that your actions or behaviors have ruined the beauty that God created you to be. Remember, we are beautiful because God created us, but if you do not believe that, then you might think that your God-created beauty can be destroyed. While you are trying to see the goodness, the blessing, and the purpose in your body and being, you can't help but see the consequences of some of your choices.

Perhaps you can relate to one of these statements from the *Created with Curves* survey:

"I've let myself go."
"My body is messed up because I . . ."

"I abuse my body because it was abused by someone else."
"I've stretched my body by overeating."[1]

Many of you feel guilt or shame because you believe that you've made bad choices with your body, whether you've overeaten or neglected, abused, or allowed others to misuse you. Furthermore, some of you feel that you can't turn things around. So we do the only thing that we know at which we won't fail: we beat ourselves up.

BEATING YOURSELF UP WON'T CHANGE A THING

In medieval times, religious zealots practiced self-flagellation (self-whipping) as a form of religious discipline. Individuals would use a whip with knotted cords and fling it over their backs repeatedly during private prayer as part of their identification with the suffering of Christ. In the most extreme cases of this ritualistic act, individuals would flog themselves until they bled. In fact, this practice still takes place in certain areas of the world today. Imagine, individuals choosing to hit themselves over and over again as they identify with the object of their worship.

As we beat ourselves in the mirror with punishing words or lack of self-care, we heap shame on ourselves. Secretly, we hope that if we feel bad enough about our behavior, then we will change. Here is an important truth: shame doesn't work. Shaming yourself never creates lasting, positive results. Shame can jump-start a behavior change, but it cannot sustain it. Shame or embarrassment might motivate us to arrest hurtful attitudes or behaviors, but moving forward in shame or embarrassment is painful, and we do not thrive.

Dr. Henry Cloud is a Christian psychologist who specializes in relationships, leadership, and mental health. You might be familiar with Dr. Cloud's book *Boundaries*, written with coauthor Dr. John Townsend.[2]

At a recent conference, I listened to Dr. Cloud talk about the concept of shame and the only way that we overcome shame. The following is a quote that has profoundly affected my life and how I conduct my relationships: "The opposite of shame is not trying to do good things. We always try to fix ourselves, but when we cannot, we feel more shame. The opposite of shame is LOVE."[3]

Stop blaming yourself for what you've allowed to happen. Whether because of gaining weight, letting your appearance fall apart, or allowing yourself to become bitter, shame isn't going to dig you out of the hole.

Furthermore, when we blame ourselves for behavior that we think we should be able to control, then we can't love ourselves. When this happens, then we start thinking that maybe God can't love us either because we are a failure in some area of our lives. Yet, here is what God says in Jeremiah 31:3: "I have loved you, my people, with an everlasting love. With unfailing love I have drawn you to myself."

God was speaking to a group of people, who happened to be His favorite people. God is speaking to them at a time when they had blown it. Big time! They stopped following God's voice and contented themselves with trying to make their own way and doing what was right in their eyes. God allowed them to experience the consequences of their behavior, and the outcomes were horrific. God's people had been enslaved, tortured, separated, downcast, and more. And yet God's love for them endured.

The same love extends to you, my dear sister. God IS LOVE. When we allow God's love to soak into our lives, shame gets squeezed out because the power over God's love crushes any shame we could feel.

Take a moment and reread this verse, but insert your name in the place where there is a blank: "I have loved you, _____, with an everlasting love. With unfailing love I have drawn you to myself."[4]

I get tingly inside when I read these words and soak them in because these words remind me of the well-worn statement: "There is nothing we can do to make God love us more, and there is nothing we can do to make God love us less."

Beautiful friend, when God's gaze falls on you, there is only love. God knows your entire story. He knows the moments of pain or horror tucked unspoken and deep within your heart. Yet, as Jeremiah 31:3 testifies, God loves you with an unfailing love.

The love that God has for you is more than enough to crush the presence and power of shame in your life. So when you are tempted to look in the mirror and see only the mistakes of your past or the last meal, be careful what you say to yourself. Anything you say that is contrary to Jeremiah 31:3 is a lie. Don't lie to yourself!

Now, look at the word *everlasting*. God's love doesn't run out. As the song by Jesus Culture says, "Your love never fails, never gives up, never runs out on me." This means that God's love endures with us through every circumstance, including the times when we make mistakes or we totally blow it.

Psalm 139:17 explains exactly what God thinks of us: "How precious are your thoughts about me, O God. They cannot be numbered!"

The writer reminds us that God thinks wonderful, precious thoughts about us. Imagine, at any moment, God is thinking "precious" thoughts about you. When you embrace that truth, it should have an impact on how you see yourself in the mirror. Not only does God love you with an unfailing love but also His thoughts about you are only good.

IN THE NAME OF BEAUTY

Let's take a moment to laugh at ourselves. Ladies, we've tried some crazy stuff in the name of beauty! One of my favorite parts of the *Created with Curves* survey was reading the answer to the following ques-

tion: "What's the craziest thing you've done in the name of beauty?"
Here are some of the funniest and most unique responses:

> I took a bath in espresso for a week because I heard caffeine
> would get rid of cellulite. It didn't work.[4]

> Duct taped my midsection to smooth out the rolls. The
> duct tape hurt coming off and the sticky part took a week to
> completely go away.[5]

> When I was in high school, I had a big acne problem. Some-
> one said if I washed my face with my first morning urine,
> it would clear the acne up. I tried it. I was desperate. I was
> also unsuccessful.[6]

REMINDER FOR THE FUTURE

Here's another powerful verse in Romans 8:1 that we need to remember when Satan resurrects our past mistakes and whispers that we
don't deserve God's love or to proclaim our beauty: "So now there is no
condemnation for those who belong to Christ Jesus."

This verse contains a promise that is accessible to those of us who
have placed our faith in Jesus Christ. We belong to Christ when we
realize that, on our own, we could not be made right with God. When
we trusted Christ for salvation, the Bible tells us that we became new
creations and old things have passed away. This means that condemnation no longer has a place in our lives.

At the beginning of this chapter, I shared a response from one of our
Created with Curves survey participants. I want you to read her story as
we close out this chapter:

> I have struggled with my weight since I was a child. As a
> kindergartener, I weighed in at 70 pounds. I have never

seen anything less than plus sized clothing. When I was 19, I was at the smallest weight of my life, a size 16/18 pants. I loved the way I felt. Then, I became pregnant and I am now at my heaviest weight I have ever been.

I do not pity myself so much anymore. I have been immersing myself in difficult Bibles studies and realize that God loves me no matter what. Now, I am learning to love myself, because I will keep abusing a body that I do not love.

I have noticed that I am invisible. I work in an office, and people literally look past me, as if I am not even there. I have received looks of pure disgust from men and women, and people go around me as if I will make them fat just by being in their air space. The opportunities that are prevalent in the company are presented first to those who are thinner than me, yet nothing stings more than the mental war.

These things hurt, and I keep close to the Lord during the various daily battles I face.[7]

If you have given yourself to Christ and asked him to be your Savior and Lord, you are never, ever condemned. You may have areas of your emotional, physical, or spiritual life that need to be addressed, but you are not condemned. So when you look in the mirror and that moment comes when Satan tries to remind you of why you can never be beautiful, shout Romans 8:1 aloud. Sounds crazy, but Satan is not the only one who needs to be reminded of those words; you do, too.

BEAUTY MARK
When we turn our futures over to Christ, we don't have to walk in shame anymore. God's everlasting love never fails us!

GROUP DISCUSSION QUESTIONS

1. List a time when you did something to your body and exclaimed the words, "What have I done?" How did you feel about yourself during that time?

2. What's the craziest thing that you've ever done in the name of beauty?

3. Why is shame so connected to our ugly struggle with beauty?

4. How can we know when we are struggling with shame?

5. Since love is the only thing that eliminates shame, what sources of love do you need to lean toward in your life? Furthermore, since God is the ultimate source of love, how do you need to lean more toward Him?

PERSONAL JOURNALING QUESTIONS

1. What are the things that make you feel guilty?

2. When do you experience shame? How does it make you feel? How has shame impacted your emotional, physical, intellectual, relational, and spiritual life?

3. Read Jeremiah 31:3. Do you believe that God loves you with an everlasting love? Are there ever times when you doubt God's love for you?

4. What's your battle plan for the next time you look in the mirror and a small voice says, "Look at what you've done to yourself"? How are you going to push back?

PICK ME

> *I will never fail you;*
> *I will never abandon you.*
> —Hebrews 13:5

Tonight, I scrolled through a few Facebook status updates and saw the following: "Feeling alone right now. Like I just don't matter."

Ever felt like that? I have.

Social media has developed into a virtual megaphone for people to express their lack of connection to the world around them. Sounding a cry for help only takes a few keystrokes.

Nanoseconds later, someone responded to this individual's plea for affirmation and encouraged her with the following answer: "Girl, you matter!!! So, so much!! Put on some happy music, find a Disney movie, call up a friend to remind you how much ya matter!!! You are the daughter of a King, that matters! You matter!"

Good stuff, right? A few seconds after the first response, another encouraging reply carried another powerful message: "You are not alone."

No one wants to be alone, yet so many of us feel lonely and rejected. We all want to belong to someone or something. The first step in belonging is being chosen. When we are not chosen, the pain can run deep.

When we don't make the team

When she chooses someone else to share her secrets with
  instead of us

When we don't get the job or promotion

When he doesn't call us (even though he TOTALLY
  PROMISED TO!)

When he decided that another woman was going to be his
  number-one girl and not you.

Our greatest fear in life is rejection, the horrific sensation that we are not good enough to be loved. This becomes a particularly sensitive area for single women who desire to find love, companionship, and marriage. This fear of rejection gets amplified when we think that it is our fault because of how we look.

I know that some of you mix it up in the club or party scene. I'm not making any judgments about clubs or mixed-gender parties, only asking you to think about what you see over the course of an evening. Do you know any particular woman who will act or dress a certain way in order to capture some guy's attention in hopes that he might choose her? Think about how behaviors can change over the course of an evening. As the magical "last call" approaches, reflect on how a friend's or even your behavior might evolve. The elusive high of being "chosen" at the beginning of the evening can turn into a standard-lowering plea of "just take me—even if I don't really matter to you."

Of course, this particular scenario doesn't have to involve the opposite sex. It can play out with friendships, especially when those friends feel more like enemies because they rarely treat you right, but having them around to mistreat you is better than staying at home bored out of your mind, right?

When we fear rejection or loneliness, we'll settle for almost anyone or anything. The desire to be number one in someone else's eye is a powerful force. No one wants to feel like she has been thrown away.

When we experience rejection that shuts the door to being chosen or belonging, we try desperately to answer the question, "Why?" Sometimes, as long as we find an answer to "why"—even if the answer is a lie—we'll accept it.

When you've been rejected, what reasons have you created to justify someone's rejection? Are you certain that your justification is even the truth? Most important, how often has rejection crushed your self-worth?

YOU'VE BEEN CHOSEN

Close your eyes and imagine yourself at the end of long line. Humor me. Maybe you're in line at the Ticketmaster box office on the morning that your favorite band's tickets go on sale. You're in line because you saved for months to purchase front-row center tickets so that you can get splashed by droplets of the lead singer's sweat. Or spit.

Only problem is that you are number 823 in line (you know this because you counted, OK), so you know that getting one of those VIP seats is impossible. But you're not leaving.

Now, imagine that while you are in line, a limousine pulls up to the curb. The chatter stops, and the crowd waits for the car door to swing open. When it does, you realize that it's the band's front man: TobyMac, Adam Levine, Keith Urban, Matthew West, Matt Hammitt, or any of the Gaither brothers—take your pick, ladies. (If I didn't list your secret crush, my apologies.)

As he steps out of the car, the crowd goes wild. At that moment, the box office window opens, and fans snap up those tickets faster than a hungry teenage boy can eat a Big Mac. As you shuffle forward, your eyes fill with tears. Those VIP tickets are going fast and you don't want to watch your dream evaporate in front of you, so you lower your head and pray that any ticket will be left. Of course, that famous singer is in the front with the lucky ones. You are not so lucky.

While your head is down, a commotion ripples through the crowd. You realize that the fans around you are reaching and grabbing toward something. As you open your eyes to the ground, there is a pair of shiny black shoes (or cowboy boots) in front of you. When you raise your head, your eyes meet his. After wiping your eyes and pinching your arm, you realize that the front man is, in fact, standing in front of you. His mouth is moving, but you can't hear. That's when you block out the din of the crowd to focus on his words: "I pick you."

"Me?"

"You."

His choice seems so improbable, so unlikely, you ask one more time: "Me?"

He smiles: "Yes, you. Would you come with me?"

You nod your head, and he takes your arm and leads you to the front of the line. Not only that, but you also receive a free VIP ticket to the show. Why? Did you do anything to deserve it? No. He didn't pick you because of what you've done or how talented you are. You were chosen just because you are you.

My beautiful sister, the central message of the Scriptures is that God wants *you*. The Bible is an enduring record of how God interacts with His people. If you don't know much about the Bible, you're likely to have questions about things like animal sacrifices and some of the strange rules people had to follow. There are parts of the Bible that it will take time to understand, but in the meantime, you need to know this: God sacrificed ALL for you.

"I AM WITH YOU"

There once was a man named Jacob whose life is recorded in Scripture. I must admit that I struggle with Jacob's story. He wasn't always a stand-up guy. In fact, Jacob's name means "deceiver."[1] He not only took advantage of his twin brother, Esau, and stole his inheritance but also gained the all-important appointment as spiritual leader of the entire family once their father, Isaac, passed away. Through trickery, Jacob secured wealth and influence.

From my human perspective, Jacob shouldn't have been entitled to blessings from God after this behavior. Only stand-up people should have good things happen in their life, right? Apparently, God has a different viewpoint.

There came a point in Jacob's life when he needed to leave home in order to get married. Jacob's family was living in a foreign land, and he was forbidden from marrying the women in that land. So Isaac sent Jacob to an uncle's house to find a wife.

One night during Jacob's journey, God appeared to Jacob in a dream. Identifying Himself by using the word *Lord* or *sacred one*,[2] God then proclaimed a special promise or covenant to Jacob. Echoing an earlier covenant with Abraham that his lineage would be as numerous as the stars in the sky, God promised Jacob that his descendants would own the land where Jacob was sleeping and that they would spread out across the earth.

I love the words that God uses to communicate to Jacob in Genesis 28:15: "What's more, *I am with you*, and I will protect you wherever you go. One day I will bring you back to this land. I will not leave you until I have finished giving you everything I have promised you" (emphasis mine).

When someone is with us, that means something. Walking shoulder-to-shoulder with someone evokes confidence and the feeling that we are not alone.

In that moment, Jacob realized that he was chosen by God for a special reason. Jacob didn't do anything to deserve being chosen; God just chose him. Even better, God promised to stick with Jacob and not abandon him.

Did you know that God chooses you? You look in the mirror and see your wrong choices, awful mistakes, shortcomings, or bad behavior, but God still chooses you. Even if you look in the mirror and only see a woman who has been brutally victimized by others, God still chooses you. He always has. Too often, we have let our life circumstances convince us that He hadn't or didn't care. Even when we reject God, He still chooses us.

The only thing worse than not being chosen is getting picked and then dropped. Oh, the pain of sharing oneself and then being abandoned. If you had a parent or spouse who walked away from your life, you know the deep, catastrophic wound of rejection. Sometimes, when we experience human rejection, we project our anger toward God. Some of us have rejected God first because we secretly fear that He will reject us. Some of you have spent a lifetime keeping God at arm's length, and guilt keeps you from drawing to Him. Know this: As long as you are living and breathing, God will not reject you once you come to Him.

Even if you have very little knowledge of the Bible or if you aren't sure what you believe about the Bible, John 3:16 should sound familiar: "For this is how God loved the world: He gave his one and only Son, so that everyone who believes in him will not perish but have eternal life."

What is it about this verse that makes it the number-one quoted verse at football games, televised rallies, or anywhere else an audience is expected? For one thing, John 3:16 affirms an essential truth that all humans need to know: God loves them. Each person is loved by a holy God who not only voices His love but also acts on it.

The next time that you are feeling lonely or unloved, instead of thinking about why you might have been rejected by others, think about a God who makes you His number-one pick every single time.

SAYING YES TO GOD'S OFFER

It's one thing to know that God loves you and chooses you, but you've got to say yes to be chosen. It's the difference between a guy saying that he wants to give you his number and you actually accepting it from him. It's the difference between telling someone that you think crème brûlée is great and grabbing the spoon to dig in for a bite.

There are lots of us who know that God loves us but have never said yes to God's offer of eternal life. You've got the head knowledge about God, but the heart connection has not been established.

If you have never done so, I want you to consider establishing a heart connection with God by accepting His love for yourself. God expressed His love for you through sending Christ to earth to die on the cross for us. You can try your entire life to be a "good enough" person, but it will never be enough. God is perfect, and His standard for us is perfection.

When we realize that God loves us and we say yes to Him, God wipes the slate clean of our mistakes, our failings, and our shame. He frees us from the penalty that comes from being human, and we become an eternally loved member of His family.

If you are ready to create a heart connection with God, you can talk to Him. You don't need fancy words or take up a particular posture. In fact, you can talk to God using this prayer:

Dear God,

I recognize that you pick me. God, I've stayed away from You for lots of reasons, but today, I want to establish a heart connection with You. Thank You for sending Christ to pay the price for every mistake or failing in my life. I know that in this moment, You have forgiven me and I no longer have to live with the shame of being alone. You have chosen me. I know this in my head and in my heart. Thank you, God.

Special note: If you've realized for the first time that God has chosen you and it's the desire of your heart to belong to God, then I would encourage you to find a good Christian friend who can explain what it means to belong to God.

BEAUTY MARK
You are always God's number-one pick.

GROUP DISCUSSION QUESTIONS

1. Did you ever endure a game or activity when you had to be picked for something? Share your memory and feelings about the experience.

2. When are some times that women long to be "chosen"?

3. What are some ugly consequences that can happen when a woman isn't "chosen" for something or by someone?

4. What does it mean to you that God has "chosen" you? To what extent do you believe that? Are there times that you have difficulty believing that God has actually chosen you?

5. If you know that God is crazy about you, what would it take for you to become more connected?

6. How could being more connected to God alleviate any fears of loneliness and rejection that you might feel?

PERSONAL JOURNALING QUESTIONS

1. What wounds do you still have from not being "chosen"? (Examples: being abandoned by a parent or spouse, having a partner abruptly end a relationship, being married to an addicted or unfaithful spouse, and so on.)

2. Is there a specific incident in your mind that reinforces your beliefs that you are not worthy of being chosen? What wrong beliefs about that situation or yourself do you need to challenge and eliminate from your thinking?

3. What are some of the unhealthy or unwise ways that you've tried to capture or keep the attention of any specific guy or men in general? (Examples: style of dress, manipulation, consuming alcohol/drugs, inappropriate body language, and so on.)

4. If you have identified any behaviors, which behaviors need to be immediately challenged and changed? What do you need to do differently?

5. Where are you at in your spiritual journey these days? To what extent are you connected with God? What are some outcomes ("fruit") in your life that support the extent of your connection with God?

6. Barb shared a number of Bible verses in this chapter. Which verse connected with you most? Why?

THE VAGINA DIALOGUE

Then the LORD God made a woman from the rib, and he brought her to the man.

—Genesis 2:22

V*agina.*
  Yes, I said it. I'll say it again: *vagina.*

Take a deep breath. I know that mentioning any part of our female reproductive system makes most women uncomfortable. But we cannot talk about our God-created beauty without discussing the parts of our body that are uniquely female. I will use some words and phrases that you hoped to never see again after junior-high sex education because I believe that our following discussion is critically important to understanding and embracing our beautiful bodies.

EVE WAS ALWAYS IN GOD'S PLANS

God is relational. Depending on what you understand about theology, you might not be aware that God exists in what we call the "trinity" or three-in-one: God the Father, God the Son, and God the Holy Spirit. In the first chapter of the Bible, we see the evidence of God's triune nature. Check out Genesis 1:26: "Then God said, 'Let us make human beings in our image, to be like us.'"

Note the word *us*. God's triune nature means that God exists as three distinct Persons, yet one God. While you won't be able to fully wrap your head around this complex theological mystery, what you should understand is that there is connectedness and community at the core of God's nature. So, as God gathered dust from the ground and breathed life into Adam's human form, the breath of life also included the need for connection and community.

This is why Eve had to be created. God knew that Adam would need community, and God chose to create another human to interact with Adam in the physical world. Instead of making a second male, God created Eve's body to perform in a manner that was complimentary yet distinct from Adam's body. Their bodies would be different, but under divine conditions, those two bodies were designed to fit together as one. While you might have thought that creating Eve occurred to God as an afterthought, God's triune nature points to His plan for Eve all along.

TURNING UP THE HEAT

Since beauty is part of God's nature and God took great joy in infusing His beauty into our world, I can only imagine the thoughtfulness that God put into creating Eve. Picture the hand of God shaping the delicate curve of her neck or shaping the contours of her hips and breasts.

Have you ever read the Song of Solomon in the Old Testament? It makes my cheeks blush whenever I read it because the scriptural author colorfully describes the beauty of the female physique. There is tremendous admiration and appreciation for the female form. In Song of Solomon 4, the man describes his bride:

You are beautiful, my darling,
  beautiful beyond words.
. . . .

Your lips are like scarlet ribbon;
   your mouth is inviting.
. . . .
Your neck is as beautiful as the tower of David,
   jeweled with the shields of a thousand heroes.
Your breasts are like two fawns,
   twin fawns of a gazelle grazing among the lilies.
. . . .
Your thighs shelter a paradise of pomegranates
   with rare spices.
(vv. 1, 3-5, 13)

Is it hot in here? What you just read is actually in the Bible. Think about how that man complimented his love. He wasn't just saying things to sweet-talk her into bed. Instead, the metaphors that he used to describe her female body were thoughtful descriptions of the most magnificent and treasured jewels, perfumes, and creatures on earth.

I tried to come up with my own descriptive version of my body that mirrors what we just read. It was tougher than I thought. In fact, I laughed so hard that I figured you might have fun with this, too. Using the passage we just read as an example, create your own positive descriptive phrases to characterize the following parts of your body:

My lips are like _____.

My neck is _____.

My breasts are like _____.

My thighs shelter _____.

As crazy or ridiculous as this exercise might seem, I hope this exercise opened an opportunity for you to appreciate some of your female features. If you struggled, that's OK. Lean into that struggle and keep reading!

As important as it is to have people in our lives uplift and encourage us, we've got to take the time to compliment and appreciate our own features.

Ladies, our bodies are dynamic, meaning that each feature of our body is multifaceted. Each feature was designed by a sovereign Creator God. Our female features were created to be attractive and to fulfill a critical purpose, essential to the survival of our human race. For example, female breasts add softness and shapeliness to our bodies, and those same breasts provide nourishment to babies. In architectural terms, our bodies have remarkable form (design) and function (purpose).

My heart breaks each time I see women who go to great lengths to minimize or eliminate any evidence of their female features. I'm not referring to women who choose to style short hair or live makeup free. I live in an area where it's not uncommon to see women who have erased any evidence of femininity in favor of looking masculine. They see their female body as a curse that must be mitigated or eliminated. But they aren't the only ones cursing their bodies.

How many of us curse our curves on a regular basis, hating ourselves for being what God created us to be? We hate our bodies for the way that our society judges us. We hate our bodies for the abuse that we think we caused but didn't. Most of all, we hate our bodies because, as much as we try, we struggle to find a way to love our bodies as they are.

Do you remember middle-school or junior-high sex education? There's only one word to describe that experience: awkward. Actually, there is another word we could use: horrifying. Even if you've left junior high far behind, it might be helpful for us to dialogue about the "why" behind God's design for our female bodies. There's a lot of drama surrounding the design of our female bodies, so I would love for you to read this section and then talk about it with some friends. You might even be able to shout *vagina* from the rooftops when you're done reading this chapter. Wouldn't that be progress!

OUR MAGNIFICENT VAJAYJAY

Who looks forward to their annual gynecological exam? If there was one area of our body that we'd love to forget about, it would be our vagina or "vajayjay," a phrase made popular by *Grey's Anatomy* character Dr. Miranda Bailey. When we think of our vaginas, we tend to operate from an out-of-sight-out-of-mind mentality.

If God created our vaginas, and everything God created is good, then what is the problem? Considering the function of our vaginas, we should be able to see the beauty of their form and function, whether or not they are currently in use. After all, this body feature is the vehicle through which life is created and life enters into the world. Unfortunately, our vaginas have become the center of our shame and embarrassment because their purpose has been perverted by our sinful world.

For too many women, our vaginas have been the vehicle for rape, sexual abuse, infertility, sexually transmitted diseases, prostitution, promiscuity, mutilation—all of these are consequences of our fallen world. When we think about it, there is an irony that our life-giving vaginas are a regular target of Satan's evil attack on women.

Here is one story of a woman who struggled to believe that she was beautiful. Growing up, this woman was told that she was nothing special and that her vagina would only be useful as a disposable vessel for men to use for their pleasure.

> I struggle with thinking that I am beautiful because my father told me from a very young age that I am not. He also told me that the only reason why someone would say that I am is because they want something from me and that men only want sex. My ex-husband would tell me that I was ugly

frequently also so it's very hard for me to accept that I am beautiful no matter if it's from a woman or a man who tells me that I am.[1]

My sisters, I know many of you have suffered from one of these consequences of our fallen world. Your vagina is not a blessing; rather it is a curse.

My prayer is that God might use this section to reframe your understanding of this aspect of our beautiful bodies.

READY TO LEARN SOMETHING NEW?

One evening, I sat down for a conversation with my friend and gynecologist, Dr. Susan Pohlod.[2] As a Christ-follower as well as former pastor's wife and nurse, Dr. Sue brings a unique perspective to our female bodies and sheds some light on the genius of the design of our feminine physique.

Dr. Sue, what is the primary thing that women forget about their bodies?

We forget that our bodies are created temples that hold God's beauty. Yet, there is a constant barrage of semi-pornographic images in magazines and media attacking our eyes and souls. These images constantly challenge and intimidate us into forgetting who we were created to be.

Last year, you and I filmed a women's health segment and there was lots of nervous laughter in the audience when you said, "Ladies, an annual gynecological exam means once a year." Dr. Sue, why don't some women come for their annual exam?

The majority of women do come in for their annual exam. Of those who don't, there are lots of different reasons. Some women are just uncomfortable. Maybe they have bad memories of cold equipment or an unfriendly practitioner. Some of my patients are in denial, especially if they have already dealt with another illness, so they don't want to come in only to find out something else is wrong. The last category of women just don't make their annual exam a priority.

What are some of the primary differences between a woman's body and a man's body that most women wouldn't know about?

There is incredible innervation in a woman's body as compared to a man's body and it—

Hold on, Dr. Sue! Explain innervation because I thought you just said innovation. Is it the same thing?

Good question. And no, innervation is different than innovation. Innervation explains the system of nerves in our bodies. So, women have incredible innervation compared to men. We have this complex spider web of nerves as compared to men. The innervation in our reproductive area is connected to our brains. This is one of the reasons why women need more time to be aroused because there are so many more physiological and emotional connections between their sexual features and their brains.

OK, let's get to some good stuff! You told me some amazing facts about our vaginas. Just amazing! What is it about our vaginas that are so fascinating?

Most women don't realize that their vagina has a memory. (My jaw drops. Dr. Sue laughs.)

Yes, our vaginas have a memory. Remember that incredible innveration? Since our vaginas have a complex system of nerves that route back to our brains, our vaginas can help us be wise and maintain good sexual boundaries. Men don't have the same system of innervation surrounding their reproductive organs. In fact, I have male colleagues who joke that vaginas actually rule the world. Our significant innervation also means that our vaginas can store information about our sexual experiences and beliefs. If a woman has experienced physical, mental, or emotional trauma (hang-ups, as a result of religion or abuse), her vagina keeps a record of that experience. This is why many women will come in for their annual exam and involuntarily tense up. I can see the muscles in the pelvic area involuntarily contract.

What do you do when that happens? How do you handle it when a woman shows signs of extreme discomfort or stress during the exam?

I encourage the woman to tell me her story. I'm not a good doctor if I'm just doing the structural stuff like exams. There are times when women need to tell their stories and share what's happened to them. When a woman has suffered trauma, I encourage her to do the work to undo the damage or else she will always struggle with poor self-esteem and she won't experience the normal sequence of stimulation well.

What are some of the questions that ladies are shy about asking when it comes to their vaginas, sex, or other reproductive-related matters?

Women in general seem very shy in how they bring up questions about their genitalia and sexual practices. There is a combination of not knowing the terms or anatomy, not knowing what is normal for their age, embarrassment about anything sexual, and, for some, religious guilt. Once I model an openness to discuss my patients' issues and assure them that it is safe to fumble through their questions, I can usually get through to the heart of their concerns.

There are a few areas that women consistently struggle to bring up in my office: sexual libido, vaginal lubrication, and urinary incontinence. Many women have questions about libido issues and have difficulty understanding that growing older does cause some changes in sexual response. Not only are there tools available to improve libido and deal with the sensitive issue of vaginal lubrication. But also it's important for wives to feel comfortable exploring creative sexual options without guilt or feeling sinful. Of course, husbands and wives must be willing participants and honor God's boundaries for marriage.

Finally, perimenopausal and menopausal women hate to discuss incontinence and often treat it as a "given" without realizing that they do not have to suffer and that incontinence is very treatable. If I don't ask in a directed way, the incontinence would almost never be mentioned!

What advice do you have to encourage women to bring up their questions with their healthcare providers?

Prior to a scheduled annual gynecological appointment, I encourage my patients to do research on any areas of concern. They can even use sites like Google to look up information and write down their questions before their office visit. Then, during the appointment, I can either validate or correct the information, then, we can go on to their personal treatment plan.

Often, physicians only have enough time scheduled for the annual medical examination. The amount of time is influenced by health insurance companies and other factors. In order to service the needs of the all of the patients scheduled for the doctor, sometimes your doctor doesn't have enough time to answer your questions. Scheduling a separate appointment for additional questions or concerns is highly recommended.

Dr. Sue, is there anything else that we should know about our vaginas?

Did you know that our vaginas were self-cleaning? Well, they are. A woman should never douche unless directed to for very specific situations by her physician!

Dr. Sue, I did not know that. Good to know. Is there anything else you'd like to say about our female bodies from your perspective as a Christian woman and doctor?

I would love to start a revolution among women, especially those in the church, to fully embrace the idea that we are temples. There is such an amazing treasure in the way that we've been created. We've been so beautifully made, and it saddens me when I realize how much time women spend comparing what they do and don't have.

BEAUTY MARK
God created the private parts of our body in accordance with the same level of beauty as the parts that we can see.

GROUP DISCUSSION QUESTIONS

1. How did your family talk about the female body as you were growing up? What were some of the words or phrases that you used to described the female anatomy? How did the words your family used shape your comfort or discomfort with your body?

2. Considering all of the ways that God has uniquely created women, is there one female-specific physical feature that you appreciate the most?

3. Which part of your female-specific anatomy makes you feel the most uncomfortable? Why?

4. Why do women hate going to the gynecologist? How old were you when you had your first gynecological exam? How do you feel now when the postcard scheduling reminder comes in the mail?

5. What part of Barb's interview with Dr. Sue about our vaginas surprised you the most?

PERSONAL JOURNALING QUESTIONS

1. Are you struggling with any shame as it relates to your female reproductive organs such as breasts or vagina? Think carefully. Can you identify the root of that shame? Was it a person, event, or cultural norm that contributed to your shame?

2. Have you ever been hurt by any harmful female-specific nicknames or derogatory terms that were directed specifically about you? What happened, and how did that incident or circumstance impact your life?

3. Look at the female-specific features on your body. Which features do you love? Which features do you loathe? Can you pinpoint exactly why you love or hate those features?

4. How much of your love or hatred for those features is generated by internal language or external feedback from others?

5. *What thoughts or beliefs about your female body do you need to challenge or reject based on what you've learned about how God has created you?*

6. *Most important, have you been to the gynecologist for your annual exam? If not, what do you need to do in order to schedule the appointment—and keep it?*

11

GOD'S PAINT PALETTE

"God shows no favoritism. In every nation he accepts those who
fear him and do what is right."

—*Acts 10:34-35*

One of my favorite television shows featured painter Bob Ross and his magical paint palette.[1] My husband and I used to watch Bob on Sunday afternoons when our children were small. Back then, Bob's mellow voice was like a balm to our tired parental bodies. Watching Bob create something out of nothing each week fascinated us. His landscapes were filled with soaring mountains, calm or turbulent skies, rushing steams, and still waters and trees, always trees.

In his calm, mellow voice, Bob would talk us through each step of his masterful plan, which was mixed and blended on the painter's palette resting in his hand. I learned about colors like yellow ochre, raw sienna, cobalt, and my favorite color, titanium white.

Each episode, I looked forward to when Bob would paint a tree. I'm not a tree-freak or anything, but Bob painted trees in a way that inspired me and reminded me of God's incredible eye for beauty. Bob knew that although trees are brown, it takes all different kinds of layered color to create a tree that would inspire a sleepy mom to stay awake a little longer. "Let's see," Bob would say. "We're going to take a little of this yellow ochre, a dab of this charcoal gray, and mix it with some of this here burnt umber. Oh, that looks nice. I think it will look even better with a little of this titanium white."

At the end of each thirty-minute episode, I soaked up the differently colored layers of Bob's landscape. Each week, Bob was able to create beauty because he understood how to combine colors to work together in harmony. Every color captured beauty because of the colors that surrounded it.

Have you ever considered why God created so many different skin colors and races? This is a fascinating question considering that He knew that we would struggle with prejudice and racism from the beginning of our human existence until now. If God is the Creator of beauty, then perhaps we might learn something about ourselves and one another if we explore why God infused different colors and physical characteristics into the human race.

The record of human history bears the scars of our struggle with race. These are uncomfortable topics that we try to avoid in polite company. Some of you might be fidgeting a bit right now. You're thinking about flipping ahead a few pages to see if, as an African American author, I'm going to make you feel guilty about being the color that God created you to be.

Friend, that's not my style.

This chapter isn't about pointing fingers or politics. I have no plans to call for a march on someplace someday. But I do think that if we come around the issue of race and process it through the lens of God's perspective on beauty, then maybe navigating the topic of race won't get bogged down in the drama of other issues.

As an African American who loves her skin color, yet who has experienced some race-related, self-image issues throughout the years, I engage in this dialogue from a biblical perspective, which helps me have healthy, loving discussions about race with friends and strangers from other races. Furthermore, as a woman who has grappled with the impact of her skin color on her ability to define herself as beautiful, I've discovered how healing and freeing it is to embrace God's truth about how and why He created the different races and cultures.

Not only do I care about walking in God's truth whenever the topic of race and ethnicity comes up, but also I want to equip you and my three daughters to walk in that truth as well, so that all of us can have confidence in a God who uniquely and specially designed a palette of glorious human colors.

THE SECRET SAUCE EVERY WOMAN CARRIES WITHIN

Have you ever heard of black-and-white twins? This category of twins happens when a woman gives birth to two children at the same time, but one child is born with brown skin and the other child is born with white skin. There have been a few sets of black-and-white twins born in the past ten years, and one couple, Alison Spooner, who is Caucasian, and Dean Durant, who is African British, has two sets of black-and-white twins, one set born in 2006 and another set born in 2009.[2] Yes, black-and-white twins are possible.

How does this happen? How is it possible for a woman with one skin color to have twins of different skin colors?

Did you know that every woman hides a "secret sauce" in her DNA? Tucked within our cells is the answer as to why there are so many different races and cultures.

While God created women with limbs, hearts, brains, and reproductive organs, He also embedded something special in the female genetic makeup—something only women possess—called mitochondrial DNA.[3]

This strand of DNA resides within our cells, specifically inside of our mitochondria. Our mitochondria are the engines that make our cells function. Our mitochondrial DNA contains genetic code that can only be passed along from mothers to daughters. This means that if a mother only has sons, her particular mitochondrial DNA strand will be lost.

Why would God insert such a particular strand within women? Think back to the beginning of human history. The Bible records the creation of Adam and Eve, followed by the stories of two of their sons, Cain and Abel. But we also know that Adam and Eve had many more sons and daughters, and those sons and daughters weren't carbon copies of Adam and Eve. Those sons and daughters had different physical features such as varied hair color and eye color, distinct facial features, and different heights. How do we know this? Well, look at the rest of God's creation documented in Genesis. Did God make all of the flowers one type? Did he make all of the animals one type? Why not? Well, because God likes diversity.

At one point in human history, God told Noah to build an ark because God was going to destroy the rest of humanity. So, Noah built the ark and loaded the animals and his family inside. After the waters receded and everyone else on earth was dead, Noah and his family disembarked, and God told him to repopulate the earth.

Question: If Noah and his family were the only survivors, then how did humanity end up with so many different ethnicities and colors? After the flood, there was a genetic bottleneck because humanity's numbers had been reduced to only a dozen or so.

This is where mitochondrial DNA comes in. This additional layer of DNA within the female mitochondria stored centuries of diversity and reintroduced it into the world even after almost every living human had been destroyed.

When God commanded Noah to go and repopulate the earth, all of the different hair colors, eye colors, and skin colors reappeared over time. The lesson we see in all of this is that God's great plan for humanity includes diversity. Not only that, but there is a purpose for this diversity.

Unfortunately, humanity has struggled to figure this out.

SETTING THE RECORD STRAIGHT

Race is one of the most controversial issues in our society. That's not news. It is embarrassing to know that Christians bear some shameful race-related history. Unfortunately, Christians and other religious groups have used the Bible to justify mistreating different racial groups.

There was a time in our human history when darker-skinned people were believed to be cursed based on an account recorded in Genesis 9. This belief was used to justify many things, such as slavery.

What was this curse about? It all goes back to an incident in the Old Testament during Noah's time. After the great flood that destroyed the earth's inhabitants except for Noah and his family, God instructed Noah to set about the process of rebuilding their lives on earth.

At one point, Noah drank too much and passed out naked. Noah's dark-skinned son, Ham, didn't handle his father's drunken condition properly. Noah became very angry and issued a curse that day in Genesis 9:25: "Then [Noah] cursed Canaan, the son of Ham: 'May Canaan be cursed! May he be the lowest of servants to his relatives.'"

Note that Ham's son Canaan was cursed. Ham was not the subject of the curse. Furthermore, since Canaan was only one of Ham's four sons, then all darker-skinned people could not be cursed. For generations, people have believed the myth that all darker-skinned people, specifically Africans, are cursed because of Ham's mistake. This is not true, but the myth evolved into a huge lie, and this lie has infiltrated and poisoned our view of race and ethnicity.

THE *P* WORD THAT MAKES US NERVOUS

Any time the word *prejudice* surfaces, people tend to get nervous. Why? Well, most of us are decent people, so we don't want to be associated with anything so unsavory. What is prejudice? I call it a "preformed negative thought." It's looking at someone and judging that person in a manner other than how God created him or her. Here's the thing: we all do it.

Some of us judge people based on skin color; others judge people based on weight or socioeconomic status. There are varying degrees of prejudice, and some forms have more of an impact than others. I'm not going to judge your prejudice, because I'm too busy dealing with my own. We have an innate desire to think we are better than someone else in some way. This myth holds us hostage, and we don't even realize it.

So, what does prejudice have to do with beauty? The core of prejudice is pride. *I'm better than you because you are* . . . Pride is ugly. It's ugly because it is an inward-focused emotion completely bent on self. God is the ultimate in beauty, and we know that God abhors pride. Pride drains and suffocates everything around it. Beauty radiates and accentuates. When we harbor hidden prejudice, we will not build relationships, we will not serve, and most of all, we cannot love.

I'm not saying that we are bad people if we acknowledge our prejudice. We live in a world in which we *all* think that we are better than someone else. We cannot experience the totality of beauty if we hold onto our prejudice. You and I have to challenge those preformed negative thoughts. How can we challenge our prejudice?

> **Acknowledge it.** List the people and places for which you either experience the at-least-I'm-not-like-them feeling or the they-make-me-feel-uncomfortable-or-afraid feeling.
> **Talk about it.** Yes, our world doesn't make it easy to talk about race, but I encourage you to start with someone who is trustworthy. Try this: "I am struggling with [insert specific situation] and I need to talk about it." Be honest with one person and go from there.

A MESSAGE FOR THOSE
WHO HAVE SUFFERED

I don't know all of the pain that many of you have unfortunately endured because you experienced racism and relentless negative comments about your skin color, hair texture, or other physical features. Some of you have not only endured the complex feelings that we have about being female but also dealt with other races and ethnicities striking out against your attempts to see yourself as beautiful.

Here's another story from the *Created with Curves* survey:

> I am a recovering ugly duckling. My twin sister is lighter skinned and was always the beautiful one. When she came to visit me at my predominantly male college, the mess hall was abuzz with the rumor that "Tyra Banks's little sister was there." I was, being much darker-skinned, quite literally, her shadow. I didn't even think I could compete so I didn't try throughout college. Something shifted when I turned 25 (it's quite a long story in some ways), and when I turned 28, I moved to Germany and my transition was complete. Something magical happened when I crossed the Atlantic Ocean, and I was suddenly beautiful in my own right.[4]

When our beautiful God infused our DNA with a diversity of skin colors, each one reflected a shade of His beauty. Unfortunately, we've been slow to realize this. Although we've sought to meet our culture's definition of beauty, we've neglected to realize how narrow that definition really is.

PRACTICAL EXERCISE:
SEEING RACE THROUGH JESUS' EYES

Whenever I see someone who looks different from me and I'm tempted to think I am better than that person—whether I think I'm better because I'm dressed better, I'm taller, or I'm just more attractive—there's an exercise that I start. It's called the "Jesus Exercise." It's very simple. When I see someone whom I might look down on or judge, I look him or her directly in the eyes and whisper very quietly one single word, "Jesus." Now, they cannot hear me say it (that would be weird), but repeating Jesus' name is a verbal cue to remind me that the person in front of me was made in the image of God. Not only that, but Jesus died for this person just like me, and in God's eyes, our value is the same. Ephesians 2:14-15 explains how Jesus came to bring unity to all of the races: "For Christ himself has brought peace to us. He united Jews and Gentiles into one people when, in his own body on the cross, he broke down the wall of hostility that separated us. He did this by ending the system of law with its commandments and regulations. He made peace between Jews and Gentiles by creating in himself one new people from the two groups."

In a world filled with race-related awkwardness, misunderstanding, and pain, it's important to know that it doesn't have to be that way! Jesus came and died so that we could live in peace. We are missing out on that harmony, but we don't have to. We can experience the peace that Jesus brings. We can find purpose and beauty in diversity, instead of division. When we see others as a reflection of the Creator God, then we understand the reason we must appreciate and embrace the spectrum of colors and cultures He created.

The solution to seeing the beauty of our different skin colors and cultures starts with Jesus. When you see someone and stereotypes invade your mind, whisper "Jesus" and let that remind you of his or her God-given worth and value. Whisper *Jesus*, and allow God to empty your heart of the fear that creeps in because someone doesn't look or sound like you. When it comes to the issue of race, Jesus is the Great Reconciler who heals our racial tragedies and brings us all together.

Perhaps this isn't a message that you need when thinking about others but a message you need to remember for yourself. Perhaps you need to whisper *Jesus* at your image in the mirror. Whisper *Jesus* to push back against the ugly memories of hateful words. Whisper *Jesus* to your reflection when feelings of inferiority or self-loathing grip your heart. Let Jesus' love overcome and overwhelm your racially charged struggles with beauty.

BEAUTY MARK
God created our unique skin colors to accentuate our beauty, not to cause us pain.

GROUP DISCUSSION QUESTIONS

1. Our comfort level with the topic of race often depends on our background and life experience. When are you comfortable talking about race? When do you become uncomfortable?

2. What was your experience with race growing up? How did your early experiences with race impact your life as an adult?

3. What did you think about the fact that God buried diversity within the DNA of women? What message does that send to us about how God feels about diversity?

4. What are some of the issues that you've noticed with race and beauty?

5. In Ephesians 2:14-15, Paul tells us that Jesus came to unite the races in him. How do you think Jesus wants Christians to handle the issue of race? What are some of the challenges that we need to navigate, especially in the church?

PERSONAL JOURNALING QUESTIONS

1. What impact has the topic of race had on your life? How has interacting with different races blessed you or made your life difficult? If you haven't had any significant interactions with people from other races or cultures, why do you think that is?

2. Is there a negative incident or experience involving a person of another race that you need to deal with?

3. What are some of the prejudices that you have when it comes to people of a different race? (Since this is your journal, this is a great place to be honest.)

4. Do you see some races as more or less attractive than others? What are some of the reasons why? Think about how stereotypes impact our perception of beauty.

5. What impressions do you think God might be putting on your heart in this area? How might He be asking you to think or act differently?

6. Is there a trustworthy person that you need to talk to about issues with race or prejudice in your past? Write down some names of trustworthy people who know you well.

CULTIVATING OUR INNER BEAUTY

Don't be concerned about the outward beauty of fancy hair-styles, expensive jewelry, or beautiful clothes. You should clothe yourselves instead with the beauty that comes from within, the unfading beauty of a gentle and quiet spirit, which is so precious to God.

—*1 Peter 3:3-4*

Have you ever run into a woman who was bad tempered, rude, or argumentative? What about a woman who complains all of the time or is greedy? It doesn't matter what that woman looks like on the outside; you don't want to be anywhere near her. Sometimes, I am that cranky, bad-tempered woman. I don't want to be, but I can be. And there's nothing beautiful about me in those moments. In fact, I'm downright ugly at those times.

In contrast, a kind, compassionate, and humble woman is like honey. Her sweet disposition will draw anyone and everyone to her. People will seek her out, and she will be valued for how good she makes them feel about being with her. No matter her physical appearance, her inner qualities leave an imprint on others souls, far deeper than the visual impression she would make on their eyes. Ultimately, she's the kind of woman who gives women a great name.

It's time for us to unpack the specific qualities of inner beauty. We're also going to discuss why and how we can apply these qualities to our lives. The main framework for defining inner beauty is explained by one of Jesus' disciples, Peter. He was writing to Christian men and women living in various areas of Asia about thirty years after Jesus' crucifixion and resurrection. This means that Peter was addressing the first generation of believers who had no religious background (which was probably a good thing) in 1 Peter 3:3-4: "Don't be concerned about the outward beauty of fancy hairstyles, expensive jewelry, or beautiful clothes. You should clothe yourselves instead with the beauty that comes from within, the unfading beauty of a gentle and quiet spirit, which is so precious to God."

In this particular letter, he addresses the community of married women who were new to faith in Christ. The women were wealthy and heavily influenced by their sophisticated, educated culture. Although these women lived in ancient times, they maxed out looking fabulous every chance they could. They competed against one another for the best hair, makeup, and jewelry using strategies that probably wouldn't be completely unfamiliar in our modern times. Like many of us, these women wanted to be admired and desired by all who saw them.

In his instruction to these women, Peter isn't being harsh or judgmental. Even though Peter did warn against wearing certain items that were associated with cultural issues during that time, he is not categorically banning beauty enhancements. Rather, he is contrasting what a woman does with her outer appearance by her own effort and what is done by God's divine gift that starts on the inside and works its way out.

Ladies, you don't have to pack up your nice clothes or cute shoes and give them away to Goodwill. Peter isn't condemning jewelry or makeup. In contrast to a façade-obsessed culture, Peter redirects their pursuit of physical beauty to inner beauty and defines the hallmarks of inner beauty: a gentle and quiet spirit.

UH-OH . . .

There is nothing small or quiet about me. Everything about me is, as my Spanish-speaking friends say, *es grande*. I'm 5'10" with big feet and a loud voice. So whenever someone taught about gentle and quiet beauty, I would feel less-than in comparison to women who appeared demure and agreeable.

At many points in life, I believed that soft-spoken, reserved women were the ideal Christian women. I thought that these women never felt the need to express an opinion and were content standing in the background. They never raised their voice, and there was an ethereal permanent smile pasted on their face. They exuded gentleness and quietness with a seemingly natural ease, and I did not. How could it be so unnatural for me? I felt like a failure.

Then, I studied and discovered the true meaning of "a gentle and quiet spirit." I exhaled with relief. It was possible for me to be demonstrative yet still reflect the "gentle and quiet spirit" that supports God's framework for a woman's beautiful nature. After studying Peter's words and other writers who chimed in on the topic of inner beauty, here is the definition that I've assembled[1:]

> **Gentleness:** Maintaining a gracious attitude, friendly behavior, and humble character
>
> **Quietness:** Choosing to possess tranquility, respectfulness, and submissiveness over worry or rebelliousness.

Instead of thinking I needed to be a shy wallflower with no opinions, I discovered that God's prescription for inner beauty was a mixture of qualities that would complement an energetic, demonstrative woman like me. Of course, I couldn't achieve inner beauty on my own, but I had confidence that God would guide me to it.

The pursuit of inner beauty is often the place where God and I meet to do business.

CULTIVATING GENTLENESS

Here's where I struggle. As a writer and speaker, I know lots of words. Sometimes, I will use my words like a four-by-four monster truck and run right over people. It's one of the things about my personality that vexes me most. You have to know that admitting this about myself on paper is painful, but authenticity should always triumph over self-preservation.

If gentleness means maintaining a gracious attitude, friendly behavior, and humble character, then the words in 1 Corinthians 13:4-5 provide a great description on how we can shape our attitude and behavior in a way that breeds gentleness: "Love is patient and kind. Love is not jealous or boastful or proud or rude. It does not demand its own way. It is not irritable, and it keeps no record of being wronged."

These verses describes the gracious attitude, friendly behavior, and humble character that I need to have toward anyone and everyone I meet.

One thing I would suggest is practicing your conversations with people in front of the mirror. Look at yourself as you imagine conversations with your friends, family, coworkers, or others. Pay attention to the words that you use and how your face looks when you use those words. If necessary, record yourself speaking and evaluate the hardness or softness of your tone. Perhaps there are certain words or phrases you need to eliminate from your vocabulary, especially if those words are contrary to the definition of gentleness.

Here's another verse along the same lines from Philippians 2:3-4: "Don't be selfish; don't try to impress others. Be humble, thinking of others as better than yourselves. Don't look out only for your own interests, but take an interest in others, too." If you are looking for more practical tips, here are a few questions that you can ask yourself before engaging in communication with others:

T—Is it True?

H—Is it Helpful?

I—Is it Inspiring?

N—Is it Necessary?

K—Is it Kind?[2]

CULTIVATING QUIETNESS

Are you a worrier? If you tend to worry, how do you handle situations that you can't control? There's nothing beautiful about a worried face that is tight and puckered. Quietness is about our choice to possess tranquility, respect, and submission over worry or rebelliousness. This is a choice we must make if we desire inner beauty!

When I get worried, I can nag in an attempt to soothe my worrying. You don't nag? Really? Perhaps you don't. But do you constantly remind, repeat, or overemphasize? It's all the same thing—even if you do it from a place of love and concern. Nagging is a form of worrying.

The first step in moving toward quietness is to stop worrying. Here is Philippians 4:6-7, verses that I may get tattooed to my wrist one of these days so that I can see them every day: "Don't worry about anything; instead, pray about everything. Tell God what you need, and thank him for all he has done. Then you will experience God's peace, which exceeds anything we can understand. His peace will guard your hearts and minds as you live in Christ Jesus."

When things aren't going our way and our hearts start to worry, our natural reaction is to try to swing things around so that we can control and fix them. In our attempt to control for our self-interest (even good self-interest), we might end up disrespecting or rebelling against others.

There are times when others make decisions and I don't like them. However, I must recognize the appropriate times and places to speak up and when to remain silent. This isn't about being a doormat. I am no one's doormat. However, I do recognize God's established chain of authority, and therefore, I choose to submit to that authority. This could be submission to my husband, boss, governing authorities, or anyone exercising the appropriate authority over me in a given situation.

Submission is a choice. If you are forced to comply, that is not submission. God's established order for humanity means that there are certain times and certain situations when others are in authority over me.

Submission is also about trust. When I submit, I recognize that I don't always have to be right, and I don't always have to have my way. God is in charge of all the details of our lives, even over and above our husbands, bosses, or other authority figures. When we show respect and deference to those God has put into authority over us, we are ultimately submitting to God.

And when we submit to the authority of an all-knowing, all-powerful, ever-present Creator God, then we will possess a beautiful tranquility and peace because we won't have to worry about anything. He will take care of us.

HOW RADIATING OUR INNER BEAUTY FITS INTO GOD'S WILL?

Some of you might be wondering how our little discussion about beauty fits into the greater context of our world. You want to know the "why" behind the admonition to develop this type of beauty.

God fits everything perfectly together by giving us a purpose that fits into His overall plan for humanity. Yet, without an understanding of how our unique design and creation as women fits into God's overall plan for the world, we won't pursue inner beauty with intentionality.

My friends, your inner beauty is the light that our dark world desperately needs. This God-cultivated beauty will draw people to you like moths to a flame. Even though things never end well for a moth drawn to a flame, those who are drawn to your God-inspired inner beauty will want to know where your radiance comes from. In that moment, you will have a platform to share about your God-given beauty and invite others to experience the same.

ABIGAIL: GENTLE AND QUIET BEAUTY IN ACTION

Our youngest daughter's name is Abigail. Her name means "father's joy." It's a wonderful description for a young lady who shares her father's tremendous compassion and sensitivity for others. My girl reminds me of another Abigail that we read about in the Old Testament. In fact, this Abigail's kindness and wisdom was instrumental in saving her life and the lives of those in her household.

Described as a beautiful woman, Abigail was married to Nabal, a very wealthy man whose name meant "fool." Even though great wealth can obscure a lot of personal shortcomings, Nabal truly lived up to the meaning of his name. Despite his cruel character, sour disposition, and rude behavior, Nabal married Abigail. It was a decision that would one day save his life.

We meet Nabal in 1 Samuel, when David had a break from running from King Saul, who was relentlessly pursuing David in order to kill him. David and his men were traveling near Nabal's property and decided to stop and ask for help.

David sent ten messengers to Nabal in hopes of obtaining food and supplies. A skilled warrior, David and his hungry and tired soldiers could have just killed Nabal's shepherds and taken the animals, food, and property that they wanted, yet David wanted his messengers to emphasize that they had come in peace and hoped to receive provisions from Nabal's obvious wealth.

Nabal blasted David's envoy with rudeness and turned the men away with empty hands. When they returned to David, their story angered him. Nabal should have known that David was the anointed Israelite king, yet David didn't press Nabal for any tributes. Offended by the foolish man's rebuff, David tells his men to prepare to attack Nabal and his property.

Back at the ranch, one of Nabal's servants ran and told Abigail about Nabal's insulting behavior. He testified to David's kind treatment of their family and warned her to expect trouble as a result of Nabal's behavior.

When Abigail realized her husband's raging unfriendliness could put their family in jeopardy, she sprang into action. After gathering generous provisions of their best food, Abigail set off to find David. Now, Abigail's actions could be construed as disrespectful because she was doing something without her husband's knowledge; however, she did not act out of disrespect. In fact, Abigail knew her actions would save her husband's family and wealth. All would have been ruined if she did not act.

When Abigail saw David and his men coming toward her, she handled herself in a manner completely opposite of how her husband interacted with David's men. Instead of acting with boldness, she adopted a humble position, bowing low before David, and spoke in a calm, respectful tone. Abigail could have made demands, or she could have berated her husband with disrespectful words, but she didn't. Instead of justifying her husband's bad behavior or speaking ill of him, Abigail asked for forgiveness.

I wonder if Abigail practiced her "don't-kill-us" speech on the way to meeting David. Did she originally plan to give a my-husband-is-an-idiot-and-I-should-divorce-him speech? Then again, Abigail could have played the victim card and jumped off her horse and thrown herself at David's feet, loudly sobbing incoherently for her life. Yet she was composed and thoughtful in her words, even appealing to David's standing as a man of God.

Abigail maintained grace under pressure, and while David would have noticed her obvious beauty, her physical features weren't the reason why he spared her family's life. Here is what David says in 1 Samuel 25:33: "Thank God for your good sense!"

Abigail returned home after meeting with David. When she arrived at home, she discovered that Nabal was partying like a king. Rather than get in her foolish husband's face and tout her achievement, Abigail remained silent about how her actions saved their lives. She maintained her gentle and quiet spirit.

The next morning, Abigail told a sober Nabal of her encounter with David. The news shocked Nabal, and he suffered a stroke, probably in realization of his foolishness and how close he came to causing the massacre of his entire family. Nabal died ten days later. When David heard of Nabal's death, he sent for Abigail, and they were married.

BEAUTY MARK
Pursuing inner beauty can have an eternal impact on your life and that of others in a way that nice legs or full lips could never have.

GROUP DISCUSSION QUESTIONS

1. Peter defined inner beauty *as a "gentle and quiet" spirit. How does his definition of inner beauty compare or contrast with our culture's idea of inner beauty?*

2. If inner beauty is supposed to be most important, then why don't we talk about inner beauty as often as we do our hips, weight, or cellulite?

3. Finish this sentence: "In order to grow in inner beauty, I . . ."

4. Why is it easier addressing issues related to our outer self versus cultivating the qualities needed in order to develop a beautiful inner self?

5. *Barb shared her inner-beauty challenge. What is your most significant challenge when it comes to developing inner beauty?*

6. *How did this group help you remain accountable to dealing with this challenge?*

PERSONAL JOURNALING QUESTIONS

1. *How would you rate your inner self? How are you doing these days?*

2. *What makes you happy? What makes you sad or angry?*

3. *In what areas of life are you modeling a "gentle and quiet" spirit?*

4. *Where are you falling short of modeling this inner beauty standard?*

STAND TALL

"Let your roots grow down into him, and let your lives be built on him. Then your faith will grow strong in the truth you were taught, and you will overflow with thankfulness."
—Colossians 2:7

The great fear of my paternal grandmother, Helen Violet Reed, was that her granddaughters would be tall. At 5'8", "Mama," as we called her, grew up under tremendous Southern scrutiny for her height. In her eyes, a proper woman simply could not be tall. When I got older, I realized Mama didn't want her granddaughters to endure the stares and comments she suffered through during her younger years.

Mama had three sons. Two of those three sons had daughters, and I am one of those daughters. Although I was small and chunky as a baby, that changed once I started elementary school. Mama often vocalized her concerns: "Oh, Barbara," she would say, "I hope you don't grow to be as tall as I am." By the time I was eleven years old, I towered over my classmates. I kept growing until my sophomore year of high school.

On one summer afternoon, Mama positioned a hardcover book on top of my head and said, "Now walk." She ordered me to walk down the length of her living room with that book on my head. For the first few days, that book spent more time on the floor than atop my head.

But Mama sat in her chair and repeated, "Now, Barbara, pick it up and try again."

She taught me to stand tall.

Before that summer, I slouched my shoulders all of the time. Not only was I tall but also shy. Being tall drew unwanted attention. Furthermore, my friends were much shorter than me, so I walked with my head down and shoulders slumped over because I felt so oversized.

Over the long summer vacation, Mama and that hardcover book trained my body to stand straight and tall. With the book on my head, I couldn't hold my head too high or too low. Instead, my shoulders had to be slightly back, and my neck had to be strong for my head to stay steady and keep the book from falling.

A first-born perfectionist, I practiced until that book stayed on my head and I could walk and turn with ease. The more that book stayed on my head, the more confident I felt.

It's no surprise that my posture is usually the first thing people notice about me—I couldn't have bad posture if I tried. Repeated practice made good posture feel natural and automatic.

I will always be grateful for the lessons my grandmother taught me that summer. However, standing tall through life's toughest lessons, challenges, and disappointments requires more than a sturdy book and practice.

HEIGHT DOESN'T MATTER; ROOTS DO

What problem could cause the world's third tallest tree to just fall to the ground after standing tall for more than one thousand years? In 1991, a tree named the Dyerville Giant[1] toppled to the ground. The 370-foot California tree was estimated to be 1,600 years old.[1]

So, why did the great tree fall? It wasn't because of a storm or natural disaster; rather the tree's root system failed. A tree cannot survive without a healthy root system taking in important nourishment from the soil around it and anchoring it deep in the ground. When a tree's root system fails, it's just a matter of time before the tree can no longer stand tall. Its support system is too weak to keep it upright.

The same goes for us. If we expect to stand tall and hold our heads high in the face of trying people or circumstances, we must have strong roots holding us up.

STRONG CONVICTIONS
EQUAL STRONG ROOTS

If we don't have solid convictions, we won't have strong roots. When we don't have strong roots, we will fall victim to the hurtful comments and negative opinions of others. Notice how I didn't say that we *can* fall victim to the comments and opinions of others; rather I said that we *will* fall victim.

Have you ever looked into the eyes of someone, perhaps a woman, who has been beaten down by words? It doesn't matter how this woman is dressed—she could be wearing exquisite designer clothes or shapeless poly-blend knit. Doesn't matter. You can pick this woman out of a crowd because her eyes lack the spark of life and her shoulders are slumped. When she walks, she shuffles her feet like every destination is against her will. Everything about her screams pain and hopelessness. She wants to disappear. Do you know this woman? Are you this woman?

Maybe you haven't been crushed like the woman we just mentioned. But every one of us has weathered negative comments about how we look or our worth as a human being. The impact of these comments varies depending on who is speaking or what is said about us.

"Oh, did you change your hair? I liked the other color better."
"You know, if you lost some weight, you might date more."

"Well, I lost my pregnancy weight before I left the hospital."

"Those wrinkles make you look so much older."

Statements like these can tear us down. How quickly can one bad comment or one bad day in the mirror wreck our self-esteem? On any given day, people may give us all kinds of unwanted feedback about who we are, how we look, or our performance. Is it possible for us to hear these negative comments and then roll them out of our memories like water off a rain slicker? Yes!

Although we cannot control the comments or actions of others, we can control what we believe about our God-given beauty, our value, and our abilities. Those beliefs become our "root system." In the following verses, the Apostle Paul provides God-inspired insight into how believers can rely on their Christ for a secure and nourishing root system rather than building shallow and sickly roots on the approval of others. Listen to the following instructions in Colossians 2:7: "Let your roots grow down into him, and let your lives be built on him. Then your faith will grow strong in the truth you were taught, and you will overflow with thankfulness."

When we have a strong foundation, when we grow by nourishing ourselves according to the teachings of Christ, we can weather tough times, difficult people, and hurtful words. That's not to say that we won't feel pain or the sting of negative feedback, but strong roots keep us resilient and allow us to remain strong.

Sometimes, we make the Christian life more complicated than it should be. In the simplest of terms, our roots are strong when we love God and love others. There are many places in Scripture when we are encouraged to love God with all of our heart, soul, mind, and strength.

When we pursue God and show our love by obeying His instructions, He gives us strength so we can stand tall and not wither under cultural or self-imposed pressure. When we have faith in God, even though our circumstances make us feel weak in the knees, we actually grow stronger. Listen to how the scriptural author describes those who have their roots firmly planted in God in Psalm 92:12: "But the godly will flourish like palm trees and grow strong like the cedars of Lebanon."

Think about a tree with a strong root system. It survives temperature changes, animals, insects, droughts, and floods, yet it survives. A tree doesn't rely on other trees to prop it up; it stands or falls based on the integrity of its roots. The same goes for you and me.

We're going to look at how God's wisdom, found in the Bible, can help you develop strong roots, just like the strong roots that anchor a tree to stand the test of time and survive year after year.

FINDING YOUR GPS

Fun fact about me: I get lost almost everywhere I go. My GPS has saved me tremendous frustration—when I use it right. The purpose of GPS is to get me where I want to go. I hate being lost because it is such a waste of time and energy.

In my life, I have what I like to call "GPS," or "God-Positioning Scriptures," to help me when I get off track or when I am overwhelmed and not sure what to do next. I like the idea of these Scriptures because I am subjected to so many messages every day about how I look or my worth as a person. Whenever I hear words that might demean, discourage, or defeat me, I ask myself: *Barb, what are your GPS verses?* Whenever I need strength or redirection, I pull GPS verses from my memory and allow God's powerful, unchanging, life-giving words to encourage and sustain my heart. Practice and repetition help make this as automatic as the good posture I learned while practicing with a book on my head all those years ago.

My favorite GPS verse is from Matthew 6:33-34: "Seek the Kingdom of God above all else, and live righteously, and he will give you everything you need. So don't worry about tomorrow, for tomorrow will bring its own worries. Today's trouble is enough for today."

Your challenge is to discover your GPS or God-Positioning Scriptures. You can have one or many—it's up to you. Pull out your Bible or use your electronic device to locate verses that remind you of how precious you are in God's sight. If you aren't sure how to use your Bible or are overwhelmed, there are a lot of verses in this book that you can highlight and memorize. For those of you who are new to the exercise, follow these steps:

1. Locate up to three GPS verses that make you feel uplifted, encouraged, and strengthened when you read them.
2. Write them down on an index card or a small piece of paper.
3. Post and memorize one verse each week until all three verses are memorized.
4. Pray and ask God to bring those verses back to your memory whenever someone (including you!) says anything about who you are or what you are worth that conflicts with God's truth about you.

If we believe that God is true, good, and beautiful, then we must believe what He says about us. If the Bible is the record of God's words, then when we memorize God's words, we benefit from the power that resides in those words. We are strengthened and encouraged. Most of all, we have the ability to reject any statement, allegation, or claim that contradicts what God says about us.

Every single one of us can have strong roots. You don't have to be wrecked by the words of others. Dig deep by holding tight to God's Word. You can be strong, and you can stand tall!

BEAUTY MARK
When you develop strong roots, you will be able to endure in any circumstance and through all seasons of life.

GROUP DISCUSSION QUESTIONS

1. Group challenge: who can put a book on her head and walk the length of a room without the book sliding off? (Have some fun with this!)

2. What can someone say to you that instantly makes you feel bad about yourself? How long does it take for you to forget about that comment?

3. If confidence is a recipe, what are its ingredients? Which ingredients are harder to secure than others?

4. When we are strong and confident in Christ, what does that feel like?

5. What are some potential GPS verses that you could write down and memorize? Share with one another.

PERSONAL JOURNALING QUESTIONS

1. On a scale of 1 to 10, how would you rate your level of confidence? If less than 5, list some of the reasons for your lack of confidence. If more than 7, list some of the reasons for your confidence.

2. Is there someone in your life who you can count on to make disparaging or hurtful remarks about your appearance or self-worth? Make a list of some things that he or she has said to you.

3. On this list put a T by the things that are true and a checkmark by the things you can control. What do you think now?

4. Finally, cross out any statement he or she has made about you that doesn't agree with what God says about you.

5. Finish this statement: "I can be confident in Christ, because . . ."

GOD DON'T LIKE UGLY

Make allowance for each other's faults,
and forgive anyone who offends you.
—Colossians 3:13

Beauty may be skin deep, but ugly goes clear to the bone.
—Redd Foxx[1]

My maternal grandmother used to say, "God don't like ugly." This statement usually followed a less-than-pleasant phone call or encounter with a friend or another woman from church. What Grandma meant was that any woman becomes ugly when she displays unfriendly or rude behavior.

I'm going to take Grandma's saying one step further and state that there is one thing guaranteed to make or keep a woman ugly: unforgiveness.

How can unforgiveness make you ugly? Stand in front of the mirror and think about the last person who made you mad. Replay your conversation with him or her. Pay particular attention to how your face looks when you repeat your portion of the conversation. Notice how much your face contorts and your lips curl. Beautiful? No.

When someone hurts our feelings or does something to us, our faces pucker and our bodies tense up. Our shoulders draw back and our fists clench. We lose the supple fluidity of our movements, our beautiful gracefulness.

Here's a quick check to see if there is someone in your life you need to forgive:

1. If there is someone whom you don't like to hear other people talk about, especially in a complimentary way.
2. If there is someone you go out of your way to avoid, even though there is nothing more he or she can do to hurt you.
3. If you hope that bad luck or misfortune happens in someone's life.
4. If you daydream scenarios in which you dominate or harm the person. (It's the dream in which you give that person a beat-down even though you've never hit anyone in your entire life.)

If you answered yes to any of these, there may be a need to extend forgiveness to someone in your life.

Unforgiveness is ugly. And, my friends, God don't like ugly.

So, we need to look at what it is about unforgiveness that makes us ugly and how to deal with it. God may intend to use this chapter to free you from an ugly place in your life or help you reconcile with a difficult person. My prayer is that you give permission to God to work in this area in your life. I hope that you know that whatever pain or anger God asks you to give up will be replaced by an infusion of God-given beauty that will blossom in you and bring incalculable joy into your life.

Think about what you know about the character of God from the previous chapters. Is unforgiveness a part of God's character? Absolutely not! In fact, these behaviors are the exact opposite of God's character, and anything that is contrary to God leads us away from God's best for us.

It might seem odd to include a chapter on unforgiveness in a book about beauty, but I suspect that for at least a few of you, God will use this chapter to do some much overdue business in your life.

For those who consider yourselves mature Christian women, don't gloss over this section with an, "Oh, I don't have a problem with this." Instead, allow God to examine your heart during this section.

WHY DO WE STRUGGLE TO FORGIVE?

Forgiveness is great, unless we're the ones who need to do the for-giving. Right now, you are thinking about the person who has wronged you and are thinking, "What! I'm not ready to set that person free! I hope that is not what you are about to ask me to do. You don't know what that person has done to me. You better back off, Barb!"

When we're angry or hurt, forgiveness feels like trying to make but-ter with a toothpick. It just seems too hard. Though we hate the pain, we don't want to let go of it until justice is done.

It might be important to clarify what forgiveness is *not*:

- Forgiveness isn't forgetting about the offense.
- Forgiveness isn't waiting for a certain period of time to pass. Time does not heal all wounds.
- Forgiveness isn't saying, "God, you forgave them. But I'm not going to."
- Most of all, forgiveness isn't forcing yourself to be in con-tact with a person who is still engaged in bad behavior and hasn't acknowledged it. You do not have to allow them to continue to hurt you.

What do we want from those who have hurt us? That's easy. We want them to take responsibility for their actions and say things such as "I'm sorry" and "I was wrong." Next, we want them to tell us how badly they feel about their mistakes and how they suffer as much as we do.

But what happens if they never step up? What do we do if they refuse to take responsibility for their misdeeds? What if the person who hurt you is dead or otherwise inaccessible? Does that mean your life is permanently damaged as a result?

It doesn't have to be that way. We can forgive. Forgiveness is setting someone free from a debt that is owed to you as a result of a wrong done against you.

A PLACE WHERE THERE ARE NO LIMITS

A group of people gathered to hear Jesus teach in Matthew 18. Jesus had just finished teaching about how to approach a person who has offended another when one of his disciples, Peter, asked a question: "Lord, how often should I forgive someone who sins against me? Seven times?" (v. 21).

In Jewish culture, a person only had to forgive another person three times. That's it. Both Peter and Jesus knew this, yet Peter also knew that Jesus operated on a different plane than the religious leaders. Perhaps this is why Peter doubled the culture's limit. Maybe he was trying to show Jesus that he could think out of the box. Turns out, Peter missed Jesus' point.

This is Jesus's response: " 'No, not seven times,' Jesus replied, but 'seventy times seven!' " (v. 22).

If you've read or heard this familiar teaching before, you know that Jesus didn't mean that we only had to forgive someone 490 times. What Jesus explained to Peter that day is that there are *no* limits on forgiveness. Just as God has no limits on forgiving us, we are not to place limits on forgiveness when it comes to others. Forgiveness should be our default plan when someone hurts us, not an option we consider.

FORGIVENESS CAN RESTORE BEAUTY

In Luke 7, Jesus was visiting the home of a religious leader named Simon. Again, Jesus didn't ingratiate himself with the religious leaders.

He made them feel uncomfortable because he cared more about heart condition than appearances.

During this visit, Jesus and the other guests were seated around the table when a prostitute, or an immoral woman as the scriptural author calls her, entered the home. Simon would have been horrified to have such a woman in his home. Everyone knew who she was and what she did. Yet this woman came anyway.

The immoral woman stopped in front of Jesus and dropped to her knees. Imagine the hush in the room as a known prostitute knelt in front of Jesus. It wouldn't have taken long for whispers to begin. In today's society, that scene would have appeared on Facebook or Twitter with updates that would have launched a thousand scandals.

Jesus sat, already knowing who the woman was and what she came to do. He didn't chase her away. Her tears dropped onto Jesus' feet as she anointed them with an expensive alabaster oil and used her hair to wipe the tears from his feet. Imagine what must have been going through her mind in those moments. Was she relieved that Jesus didn't chase her away? Was she grateful that he didn't try to use her as other men did? All we know is that her tears reveal how deeply moved her soul was in that moment.

The significance of the woman's actions was lost on Simon, who wondered if Jesus knew what kind of woman knelt in front of him.

Jesus heard his thoughts. "Simon," he said to the Pharisee, "I have something to say to you."

Jesus told the story of a man who loans fifty pieces of silver to one person and five hundred pieces of silver to another. Neither man could repay the debt, so the man forgave both debts. Jesus closed his story with this question: "Who do you suppose loved him more after that?" (v. 42).

Then, Jesus pointed out that Simon may have invited Jesus for dinner but did not treat him as an honored guest. The immoral woman honored Jesus in heart-felt ways that revealed her true desire for forgiveness. So after asking that question, this is what Jesus said to Simon: "'I tell you, her sins—and they are many—have been forgiven, so she has shown me much love. But a person who is forgiven little shows only little love.' . . . And Jesus said to the woman, 'Your faith has saved you; go in peace'" (vv. 47, 50).

Imagine how it must have felt to be that immoral woman, now a forgiven woman. She stood up, free from the burden of being a prostitute, a woman who was deeply aware of how flawed and sinful she was. She was forgiven! Could you imagine the smile on her face and the light in her eyes? There's nothing more beautiful than the look of joy and freedom on someone's face. The tremendous burden of sin was lifted from her heart, and once it was removed, the beauty that God created her to be shined through.

Peter only understood a forgiveness that had limits. But the immoral woman came to Jesus hoping and praying that there was enough forgiveness for her and all of the mistakes she had made. Do you want to live in a world where there are limits to the forgiveness that you can receive? If not, then should you place limits on the forgiveness that you are willing to extend to others? Colossians 3:13 is a verse that each one of us must remember in order to navigate our relationships with others: "Make allowance for each other's faults, and forgive anyone who offends you."

Here's the lesson that we need to remember about forgiveness: our capacity to forgive is directly related to our understanding of how much we have been forgiven.

Who haven't you forgiven? Is it a family member who hurt you long ago or the office colleague who just gets on your nerves every day with her rude comments? When we don't practice forgiveness, each offense becomes like a brick wall in our heart. Brick walls can be protective, but they can also be barriers. Some of you have a barrier built in your heart.

You've been hurt so much by so many people that you've built a brick wall twenty feet high.

It doesn't have to be that way. You can forgive.[2]

How can you know when you've forgiven someone? Here are three clues:

1. You think of that person's name and pray God's best for him or her.
2. You don't get jealous or angry when others speak of that person.
3. You can pray for that person and ask God to bless him or her.

You can make the decision to forgive. It won't be an easy decision, but each time you think of the person who offended you, choose to speak the words "I forgive you" in that moment. Each time you speak those words, you chip away at the pain and anger. Each time you speak forgiveness, you tear down the bars that the prison of pain wants to build around you. Forgiveness opens your heart and allows your beauty to shine through.

GRANDMA'S STORY: HOW HER FORGIVENESS CHANGED OUR FAMILY

When I was a kid, my maternal grandmother suffered from poor health after divorcing my grandfather. Most of my memories of her during my early years were of visiting her in the hospital.

As an adult, I found out they divorced in part because of my grandfather's unfaithfulness to my grandmother. Grandma's pain and devastation turned to anger and bitterness. She suffered from bleeding ulcers for many years until she decided to forgive my grandfather. Then she got better.

One day, when I was about nine years old, I entered my grandmother's home, and she immediately said, "Shhhh!" My grandfather was sleeping in her bedroom. Apparently, he had had surgery but could not convalesce in his tiny motel room, and there wasn't enough space for someone to come and stay with him. So my grandmother took him in and cared for him.

In the years that followed, Granddaddy would stay with Grandma a few more times. His hips were deteriorating, and he was unable to move out of the bed or care for himself. During his stays, Grandma moved into my aunts' small, shared bedroom.

For many years, my grandfather's health was much improved. He leased a new apartment across town, but he would come to our house each day to hang out with my uncle in my dad's garage. Granddaddy was always busy. Each morning during the summer, he would go fishing and bring back food. Other times he oversaw our chores or drove us to sports practice. During those years, we had the chance to build a relationship with our grandfather, which we couldn't have done if Grandma wouldn't have forgiven him.

After I grew up and started a family of my own, my grandfather's health began to deteriorate again. The doctors decided after multiple infections to completely remove my grandfather's pelvic bones, rendering him wheelchair bound for the rest of his life. Interestingly enough, Granddaddy could still stand for short periods of time when needed.

My mom and her sisters were Granddaddy's primary caregivers, but Grandma checked up often to make sure they were doing a good job. She cooked Grandaddy a meal once a week and dropped it off. She also dyed his hair. He had red hair and hated it. So, once a month or so, Grandma would drive over to his apartment and dye his hair black again.

Grandma's decision to forgive Granddaddy changed him. I never knew anything about the conversations they had about what happened. I know there were a few blowups and some periods of time when they didn't come around each other. But I do know that Granddaddy watched out for Grandma. If he found out that her car needed tires or repairs, he would slip my mom or aunts money toward the cost. During the holidays, he would never buy Grandma a gift, but I'd overhear him whispering to my mom about getting Grandma something nice for Christmas from her and her sisters.

I always appreciated the fact that Grandma encouraged us to have a relationship with Granddaddy. There were lots of lessons that we learned from Granddaddy, and I've passed along many of those lessons to my children.

Grandma could have bad-mouthed him for what he had done, but she didn't. When Granddaddy passed away, Grandma was proud of the fact that she considered him to be a friend. She said: "The best decision I ever made in my life was to forgive him."

My grandma's example of forgiveness taught me that we have the power to heal people and relationships when we choose to forgive. It's a lesson I've never forgotten.

A FEW WORDS ABOUT RECONCILIATION

There is a huge difference between forgiveness and reconciliation. Misunderstanding the two can actually prevent someone from engaging in the forgiveness process.

> **Forgiveness:** Setting someone free from a debt that is owed to you as a result of a wrong done against you.
> **Reconciliation:** The process through which broken relationships are restored.

There are conditions and rules for reconciliation. Don't misunderstand this: God desires reconciliation. We know this because the Bible tells us that God's desire is to reconcile the world to Him. However, our human choices sometimes get in the way of this. Here are some of the conditions for reconciliation:

- Reconciliation requires willingness of all of the parties involved.
- The bad behavior should have ended, and each party should have an assurance of safety.
- There is to be a desire for all sides to come together.
- Each party has to take responsibility for their behavior or actions.

IF RECONCILIATION ISN'T AN OPTION

There are some situations when reconciliation isn't going to be possible or wise. There are other times when reconciliation doesn't work out because the other person just isn't ready yet. In that event, here is my go-to verse for dealing with difficult personalities and relationships from Romans 12:18: "Do all that you can to live in peace with everyone."

I love this verse because it identifies what I am in control of: me. I can't make people do what I want them to do, but I can control how I will respond to difficult people. When I handle myself well, God's beauty shines through. So, here are some general guidelines if reconciliation isn't possible:

- If the person is still engaged in bad behavior, forgive him or her and extend grace. But maintain good boundaries. Limit your time around him or her and be wise.
- If you are the offender and the person you've hurt isn't interested in reconciling, then do what you can to live in peace and not frustrate or manipulate that person into reconciling before he or she is ready.

BEAUTY MARK
When we forgive, the beauty of that forgiveness overflows to everyone around us.

GROUP DISCUSSION QUESTIONS

1. What is so ugly about unforgiveness? What are some of the ugly feelings associated with unforgiveness?

2. Share a story of a time when you forgave someone who hurt you. How did you know you had forgiven him or her?

3. One of the main points in this chapter is that we forgive according to the understanding of how much we've been forgiven. What does that statement mean to you?

4. When do you struggle with forgiveness?

PERSONAL JOURNALING QUESTIONS

1. Make a list of the people in your life whom you haven't forgiven. Write down one or two words next to their name describing how you feel about them or what they did to you.

2. Now, make a list of what you've done to hurt or offend others.

3. Compare the lists. What are some of the differences between the lists?

4. Think about Jesus and the immoral woman. When we have a self-righteous attitude like Simon, we pick and choose who deserves forgiveness. Who do you need to forgive but don't want to? What are some of the reasons why?

5. *What are some of the reasons that you need to forgive? How will forgiveness impact your life?*

6. *If you are ready, write out your declaration of forgiveness in this journal entry. The subject of your forgiveness doesn't have to be present for you to engage in the forgiveness process.*

WHAT WE'LL GIVE AWAY FOR LOVE

So now there is no condemnation for those who belong to Christ Jesus.

—*Romans 8:1*

I can't pinpoint when or why it started, but I learned that it was my sexuality that was going to take me places. So, if I wanted a boy to like me and I was desperate for that—to call me beautiful, to say the right thing—it left me in the position to give myself away for love.

—*Allison*

Honey, God took you from the pole to the pulpit." These were the words that Allison's husband spoke to her a few years ago. After decades of searching for affirmation, acceptance, and love in places filled with heartache and regret, Allison realized that God could lift her from the pit of guilt and shame and allow mercy and redemption to rain down on her life.

If you have ever wondered if it was possible to wander so far from God that He couldn't bring you back, then Allison's story is for you.[1]

My parents divorced before I was four. My mom remarried when I was ten, and by the time I was twelve years old, I drank regularly. I had my first shot when I was about eleven with my mom at a bar. It wasn't a big deal for me to have a drink. I remember drinking beer at home even earlier than that. I would drink during the week and then go to church to learn about God on Sunday. I caught on to the idea of hypocrisy pretty early.

I was thirteen years old when a family member began to involve me in her adulterous sexual exploits. She would wake me up in the middle of the night. We would go meet up with her lover at a hotel. I was told to go to sleep on the floor, while she would have a sexual liaison with the man in the bed above me.

At the end, she would take me shopping for new clothes before we headed home to keep my silence. These situations began to reinforce the idea that sexuality could get me things.

Around the time I started formulating ideas about how sexuality worked, I also began to feel the struggle that came from being compared to others. As early as nine years old and into my early teens, I have vivid memories of standing next to my cousins and being judged by adult female family members. Their commentary was blazed into my memory:

"Her breasts are bigger than so-and-sos."

"She has a prettier smile."

"Her attitude is so much better."

"She's maturing faster. Did she start her period?"

Oddly enough, this scenario seemed normal. In my world, it was normal to worry about what other people think of me. It was OK to want people to like me. In order to be found acceptable, I wondered about how to make my boobs bigger (even though I was well-endowed for my petite frame) or how often I needed to suck in my gut so that I could appear thinner.

Those comparisons created a lot of problems between my cousins and me. We were friends, but once we were pitted against each other everything became a competition. Boys became the prize we would fight over.

Home life wasn't always peaceful. My family fought a lot. My mom's escape was to call the police. Our fights were always about the disparity of our lives—the inconsistencies between who we said we were and how we were actually living. I knew something was wrong, and as a kid, my survival response was to fight, although flight was very real in my life as well. Alcohol provided an escape. I didn't have to feel. I didn't have to remember.

I started high school very young. I was thirteen. However, I had life experience far beyond my years. I drank regularly. I only dated guys who were older and even some out of high school. If I dated a guy who was still in high school, I made sure he didn't go to my school because I didn't want the drama or a reputation.

TWO LIFE-CHANGING EXPERIENCES

During Allison's sophomore year of high school, two pivotal life experiences occurred that further shaped her experience of self-worth. The first experience was when Allison lost her virginity when she was fifteen years old. This first "real" boyfriend was eighteen, and she was "in love." However, the relationship was manipulative from the beginning and turned extremely violent before it ended.

The second pivotal moment happened when a family member arranged for fifteen-year-old Allison to do a striptease in front of a classroom full of college students.

I wanted to go to college. However, I knew my parents wouldn't pay for it, so I decided that I would become a stripper to pay for college. My mom said that since I had a body for it so why not do it and pay my way through college.

That same year, a family member gave me an opportunity to strip for the first time and arranged for it to happen. I showed up to a classroom of college students with a boom box and stripped right on down to a see-through black fishnet teddy—for all intents and purposes I was naked in front of thirty-plus strangers. It wasn't until much later in life that I realized that situation was actually an act of child sex trafficking.

In the midst of this craziness, I still went to church. Even more, I would teach Sunday school, but I felt so conflicted because my life seemed so divided. There would be months of feeling so close to God, but then I would make a mistake, feel unworthy, and look for acceptance elsewhere. When I bottomed out of a cycle, I would melt down and come back to God. For all of the scripture my grandparents and the church taught me. I had a lot of head knowledge about God but never learned how to make it real. I could get God's unconditional love for other people, but it couldn't possibly be for me.

I went through several broken relationships in high school. I went to church, worked at the mall. I would tell myself, "Allison, be a good girl. Act right. Look good." But, it was hard because I was never good enough and incomplete with a man.

Allison's senior year of high school was a blur. She spent most of the time drinking and hanging out with her friends and college guys. She didn't have tons of sexual partners, but no relationship had any real meaning. You couldn't even call them "relationships." She was like a party favor—a prize to have at the end of the night. Her sadness, loneliness, and pain combined with alcohol created plenty of opportunities for those guys to take advantage of her sexually.

LOOKING FOR LOVE AND MAKING BIG MISTAKES

I always knew I could never measure up to people expectations. I often asked myself, "Why can't I be better?" Then, at other times I wondered, "God, how can you love someone like me?" But knowing I couldn't measure up never stopped me from trying.

My mom would tell the folks at church to pray for me and give them her view of my misdeeds. So when I came to church, I knew people were thinking badly of me—and they weren't shy in telling me what they thought. Growing up in the church I watched people judge my mom for her choices, and now they judged me.

I stopped going to church except at the holidays. I wasn't against God, but I couldn't see how church could help me. I didn't want to walk in and feel the shame anymore. I was full of anger and hurt, frustrated because I didn't understand how God was a God of love and yet I couldn't truly find it.

Once Allison graduated from high school, her parents told her she was on her own. She worked from the time she was eleven years old. After graduation, she got a legitimate job, where she would eventually meet her future husband. Before that, though, there was one particular incident that would bring Allison to a new low.

> A nearly thirty-year-old coworker asked me to hang out with him and some of his friends. I agreed. After a night of drinking he and I ended up in bed together. That didn't shock me. I had learned over and over what guys wanted from me. But that next morning, I woke up in what I thought was his apartment. It wasn't. The door opened, and a woman with small children walked in while we were lying there, just waking up, wondering why he never came home. As I lay there, I asked myself, "What did I get myself into? How did I let this happen?" I didn't know he had kids, or that he had a wife because the fact was I didn't really know him other than at work. At that point, I realized that I was no better than the family member that took me along for her adulterous escapades. I was becoming the very thing that hurt me years before. And that realization stung my heart.

After that incident, Allison made the decision within herself to find a long-term committed relationship and stop letting guys use her as a prize. She turned her full attention to a shy man at work whom she would chat with every night, and just a couple of years later, he would become her husband. At first, she didn't think he was interested in her, but eventually he asked her out. Like her other relationships, this one also became sexual at the very beginning. As she was experiencing this new love in her life, Allison also began a new job: stripping at a local club.

LIFE IN THE STRIP CLUB

At the beginning of the night, the dancers are paraded out on stage in front of the customers during what was referred to as a "cattle call." I loved this part of the night because people would cheer and holler, telling me that I was beautiful and desirable—and they were willing to pay for my attention. It was an adrenaline rush. I had value because I had a price tag.

For a girl with my history, I believed I for once had power. I said when and who. If I didn't want to dance for someone, I didn't have to. There were rules that they couldn't touch me, and I followed them. However, someone was always telling me what to wear, how to fix my hair, how to look better so that I could maximize the amount of money I was making for the club. As much as I thought I was in control, I really wasn't.

By this time, the dream of college had already been crushed. It's not possible to strip for eight to ten hours, drink all night, and wake up to attend class, do homework, and get ready before doing it all again. But I felt some kind of value and worth and I was "all-in." I began working towards the goal of traveling to other clubs on the circuit and to be a centerfold in magazines.

That first year I had to work on Easter, and I wasn't able go to my grandma's for dinner. In the sex industry, you get stage names, but on that Easter Sunday, as I was walking off stage, I heard my real name. My dad walked over to me, while I was completely naked, and said: "What the **&#^ are you doing?" I replied, "I'm working."

There I was standing completely naked in front of my dad. It was an embarrassing moment. He didn't say a word. Yet he didn't seem angry that I was stripping; he was angry that I missed Easter dinner. After yelling at me, Dad stayed to watch several of my friends dance.

THE NEED TO CHANGE

A year after she started dancing, Allison—still with the shy man from her previous job—got pregnant. It was an unplanned pregnancy, but Allison said they knew that together they would raise this baby. However, pregnancy didn't stop Allison from stripping until she was eight months pregnant. Then, she switched to working as a bartender in the club.

After her child was born, Allison went back to dancing and spent almost another year in the industry with many cycles of quitting and starting back up.

One day, Allison looked into her baby's eyes. That's when she realized she needed to change.

> The emotional damage and baggage that led me to the sex industry was the same baggage that kept me going back. I didn't think I was good for anything else.
>
> I wanted more for my baby than the life I was living. I dreamed bigger for my child than I could for myself and I never wanted my child to live like I had. Then there was a moment when I finally asked myself this question: "If it wasn't good for my baby, then how could it be good for me."
>
> I realized that I couldn't do it anymore. I couldn't keep showing myself to anyone and everyone who would give me a buck.

Again, Allison realized how God was working in her life. She had married her boyfriend by this time, and he had started a new position that paid well enough for her to make a clean break without creating a financial hardship for the family.

Once she quit dancing, Allison decided to go back to church.

> Each week after the sermon was over, I went to the altar calls with the same desperate prayer: "God, I am so sorry.

I really messed up. Here I am again. Please forgive me, forgive me, forgive me."

At one point, I realized that I probably should talk to someone about what I had been through. So, one week, I told a woman at the church about everything, including the drinking, stripping, and getting pregnant before I was married. After telling her my story she said, "How could you call something done in sin a gift from God?"

The brokenness inside me believed she was right. Again, I asked myself, "How could God love a broken person like me?"

Allison left that church. Eventually her husband came to Christ, and they found a church they could attend together. This time, however, Allison kept quiet about her past.

I took all of the tangible stuff from that period of my life and put it in a box on the top shelf of the closet, including copies of a magazine that I posed in, my outfits, and pictures from the club.

That box became my whipping stick, and anytime I opened my closet door it would remind me that no matter how far I had come—no matter how hard I had worked to become something different that box reminded me of what I was.

I kept my mouth shut about my story, especially at church. I would admit backsliding, but that's it. I made sure I looked good, dressed good, and smelled good, and then people would like me. I played the good mom, good wife, sang in the choir, and as long as I did all of that, I didn't have to admit my past.

SEEING GOD DO NEW THINGS
AND HEAL THE PAST

In 2005, Allison sensed that God was calling her into ministry, but she had no idea what to do. She began serving in the nursery and singing on the music team. There was even a thought that she might go back to school. Allison had managed to get her bachelor's degree in 2003, but she didn't want to get a master's degree. However, her pastor suggested that she might pursue an online master's degree in ministry. Allison enrolled in the program but refused to entertain the idea that she would ever be a pastor.

> My entire life I was told that I couldn't be a pastor or a missionary because I was a woman. And then there was my past. Who would want someone with my past as their pastor? Yet I prayed, "God, since I don't know what I am doing, I will follow you."
>
> I finished my master's in 2009 and preached my first sermon in Virginia. When I finished that forty-five-minute sermon, I realized that what had just happened had nothing to do with me and everything to do with Him. I apologized to God: "I'm sorry for telling you what I was not going to do."

Even though Allison had her family and her education, she still carried the scars of her hidden past. Allison worked hard to kill off the memory of the girl who danced naked in the club because she didn't believe that there was anything redeemable about those memories.

> In summer 2008, I took that box out of my closet and dumped the contents into a fire pit in our back yard to burn it. It was an act of defiance, not surrender. It was like I was saying, "God, you can't fix her. But I can destroy her."

It was raining while I was outside and the strangest memory came to me. I remembered being in the club, sitting next to the stage waiting for a cattle call, and it felt like someone was spitting on me. I remember telling the girl next to me to stop spitting on me, but she said it wasn't her.

As the rain was falling that day in my backyard, I remember God whispering, "Allison, that was me. Those droplets of water were my tears for what you were going through. I was there with you during that entire time. I never left you."

Yet, even after that revelation, I still walked away from the fire pit believing there was nothing God could do to fix or redeem that girl.

About six months later, a former stripper friend contacted Allison on Facebook. However, Allison didn't want to respond because that part of her life was over, and she didn't want to open that door again. But Allison realized that because she was now a pastor, she could help that woman. So, they started getting together to talk.

I realized that she didn't need me. I needed her. In those six months, she got me to a place where I could talk about my life as a stripper and it was a safe place to remember.

We talked about what we had lost through that experience. During those conversations, God was opening my heart and he was slowly resuscitating the girl I tried to murder the day I burned the box. That girl was me. As much as I didn't like her, she was a part of me.

In the months that followed, God would show Allison a new vision for how she could minister to women who were walking a road she had traveled. That June, Allison went to Florida when her child competed in a Bible competition. While there, Allison had the opportunity to attend a number of workshops.

One of those workshops was about "organic churches" that meet the people where they are. These churches aren't concerned with buildings or money, just with creating spaces where people could be transformed by God.

After having a conversation with the workshop instructor, Allison realized that God was leading her to be a missionary in the adult entertainment industry. But, before she could do that, Allison had to allow God to complete the healing in her life.

> I opened my Bible one night and wrote out every verse that had to do with love and redemption. I finally understood Romans 8:1: "There is no condemnation for those who are in Christ."
>
> I realized that when I killed that girl inside of me, I stopped myself from forgiving myself. I stopped God from bringing healing to that place in my life. When I realized that what I was is not who I am, I was free to embrace that I was a child of God and that never changed. God was with me in the hotel room as a little girl. He was with me when I woke up in places where I never wanted to be and even when I woke up in places where I didn't know I was.
>
> As I shed the guilt and pain, I could look back and see the places where God was there by my side—loving me, providing for me, and protecting me. All along, it was me that chose to carry the mantle of shame and guilt. It wasn't Him.

From that place of healing, Allison had a vision for an organization that rallies around women who are employed in the sex industry. Allison wants the women to realize they are free to become the women

God created them to be. But, if they are not ready yet, she will not heap shame or guilt on them. She just wants to be there and be a part of the deep work that God wants to do in their lives.

In addition to working as a pastor in a local church, Allison works with a team of volunteers to create gift packages to distribute to the women working in the strip clubs. These gift bags, filled with toiletry items, books, lotions, or anything that a woman might like, are handed out with no strings attached. Allison's hope is that, in addition to being a way to share her story and the gospel of Christ, the gift bags will be a bridge to establishing relationships with the women in hopes of helping them see their self-worth.

BEAUTY MARK
Even if your life has gotten way off track, you can never travel too far away for God to forgive you and redeem your mistakes.

GROUP DISCUSSION QUESTIONS

1. Where did you connect with Allison's story? If you don't feel your connect with some aspect of her story, do you know someone who does?

2. What were some of the warning signs during Allison's childhood? Did you experience any of those warning signs? What could have happened that would have made a difference in your life?

3. Allison talks about the hypocrisy of going to church but not living out at home what the Bible says. Yet, what were some of the "seeds" that were planted in her life?

4. At one point, Allison decides to share her story with someone at church. However, it was a disastrous experience. Why do people in the church have difficulty handling stories like Allison's? What are some ways that churches can be a safe, healing place for people with stories like Allison's?

5. If someone approached you with her story, how would you handle in a way that reflects the character of God?

6. How did God redeem Allison's life experiences?

PERSONAL JOURNALING QUESTIONS

1. Think of your ugly struggle with beauty. The path to winning our struggle isn't a straight line. Sometimes, we make progress, and at other times, we experience setbacks. How are you doing these days? Where are you "winning"?

2. Allison's story reminds us that we can never go too far from God. He longs to forgive us and redeem us. Where do you struggle to believe that God can redeem your mistakes?

3. What are some of the ways that God might be able to use you in order to bless other women who have struggled in similar ways as you?

JUST LIKE EYEBROWS, TWO ARE BETTER THAN ONE

Two people are better off than one, for they can help each other succeed. If one person falls, the other can reach out and help. But someone who falls alone is in real trouble. Likewise, two people lying close together can keep each other warm. But how can one be warm alone? A person standing alone can be attacked and defeated, but two can stand back-to-back and conquer. Three are even better, for a triple-braided cord is not easily broken.

—Ecclesiastes 4:9-12

There was the time when I tried to wax my own eyebrows. I ended up with "angry" brows because I did it wrong.

—Created with Curves *survey participant*[1]

When I was thirteen, I sang in the youth choir at my small Baptist church. My grandmother was the pianist and director. There were a dozen or so of us kids aged ten to fifteen, and Grandma taught and fussed at us each week during choir practice until we got the songs prepared just right for Sunday.

One Sunday afternoon, our church was hosting another church for an afternoon program. It was a big deal to host another church from out of town, so we had to be on our best behavior. Grandma wanted our little youth choir to look good, and she wanted us to sound good.

Of course, Grandma wanted to look good, too.

Earlier that morning, however, Grandma had an accident with one of her eyebrows. Her eyebrows were always plucked very thin, and she would fill them in with a pencil. However, on that particular morning, Grandma couldn't find her tweezers, but there was a razor handy. I'm not sure how everything went down, but the bottom line was this: Grandma accidently shaved off one of her eyebrows.

Then, she shaved off the other because she didn't want to have only one natural eyebrow. Her plan was to draw them both back on with her black eyebrow pencil. Except, she couldn't find it.

My girlfriends and I were in the choir room putting our choir robes over our summer Sunday dresses when Grandma rushed in with a frazzled look on her face.

"Girls, do any of you have a black eyebrow pencil?"

We were thirteen years old. None of us plucked our eyebrows yet.

"No."

"Oh, no!" exclaimed Grandma. She rushed over to the mirror on the sidewall. "I need a black eyebrow pencil, girls. My brows are gone."

I stepped across the room toward my grandma as she looked in the mirror. Yes, indeed, Grandma's brows were gone.

One of my friends spoke up: "Miss Magnolia, I've got a navy-blue eyeliner. Will that help?"

"Quick, give it to me."

Grandma took that blue eyeliner pencil and drew on a set of new eyebrows. They were navy blue eyebrows, but Grandma would be wearing a navy blue choir robe, so it seemed that things had worked out. Almost.

An hour later, our little youth choir took the choir stand and was singing away. It was a really hot afternoon, so we kids were starting to sweat. So was Grandma. She jammed those fingers over the piano keys like her life depended on it. Every now and then, she would raise one hand while playing in order to emphasize a note we were singing. We sounded great!

As we moved into the second song, we sweated even more. Grandma was sweating so much we could see the perspiration running over her new navy blue eyebrows and down her face.

That's when it happened.

As I clapped in time with the music, I looked down to see my grandmother raising her hand toward her face.

Noooooo!!!!

It was a like a slow motion scene from a movie. I watched as Grandma pulled her hand across the top of her forehead, wiping away the sweat and one of those navy-blue eyebrows.

I don't remember if I kept singing or not. My girlfriends also saw it happen and started to giggle between breaths while singing. I remember looking at my beloved grandma, who didn't know that she was pouring her heart out on that piano with only one eyebrow.

Yet, Grandma played on. Her one blue eyebrow raised, then crinkled, when she saw the other kids giggling, but that only made them snicker more.

A few minutes later, I saw more beads of sweat rolling down her face. Then, I saw her other hand go up toward the other side of her face.

Oh no! Not again!

Um, yes. Grandma pulled her other hand across the other side of her forehead, wiping away the remaining blue eyebrow.

I was horrified. Then, I laughed.

And Grandma got mad. When we finished that final song, we exited the choir stand, and Grandma ushered us back into the choir room to fuss at us for our behavior. At one point, we got her to look in the mirror to see why we were laughing.

Then, it was Grandma's turn to laugh. Two eyebrows are definitely better than none!

THERE IS SAFETY IN NUMBERS

What do you talk about when you are hanging out with a group of girlfriends? One of the best parts about being a woman is the chance to get together with other women and talk about anything and everything. If you are on a journey to live as the beautiful woman God created you to be, you cannot sustain this journey without other women walking by your side, to challenge you and encourage you to keep going.

Reread the verses from Ecclesiastes at the start of the chapter. Think about the words in the context of your struggle with beauty and the importance of having people in your life to help you through this particular journey.

In the Old Testament, the Israelites fought a group of foreigners while their leader, Moses, watched the battle from the top of a hill. As long as Moses held up his staff, the Israelites had the advantage. When his hand dropped, the advantage would shift to their enemies.

It was a long battle and Moses' arm and hand grew tired. His two brothers, Aaron and Hur, found Moses a rock to sit on, but Moses still struggled to hold the staff high. Then Aaron and Hur did something that made all the difference: they stood on each side of Moses, grabbed his weary hands, and used their strength to support him in what he needed to do.

Ladies, we find ourselves in a battle every day when we look in the mirror. It's a battle for us to see God first instead of our flaws and imperfections. It's a battle to forgo flaw finding and choose to embrace God's truth, His goodness, and His beautiful nature as our own. This is not a battle we can fight alone. We need other women to come alongside of us when we are tired or feel defeated to hold us up so that we don't despair.

Do you have those women in your life?

WHEN WE STRUGGLE WITH OTHER WOMEN

How many times have you heard a woman say, "I don't trust other women," or, "Guys make much better friends than women"?

Some women struggle with their relationships with other women. Here's one Christian woman's response: "I don't have a bestie, a good friend, maybe 'frenenemies' at work at best. I am in small groups but don't really feel I belong."[2]

There is a difference between knowing lots of people and being connected. Connection happens when we allow ourselves to be known and we get to know others. Some of you avoid this connection out of fear; others just don't think you need a close connection.

Belonging is essential, but it shouldn't be exclusive. Our lives shouldn't be about looking for that perfect "bestie" and endangering current relationships in the process. Sometimes, we overanalyze our relationships with one another, don't we?

"When's the last time I talked to so-and-so?"
"Do I need to call her?"
"Why isn't she calling me?"
"Is she mad at me?"
"Why did she say that on Facebook?"
"Should I apologize?"
"Why isn't she calling me to apologize?"

It's no wonder we can tire of the drama of being friends with other women!

Too often, we are preoccupied by how other people treat us, and we don't always focus on our personal responsibility in relationship. It's easy for us to live by the "what have you done for me, lately" friendship motto rather than the "ask not what people can do for you, rather ask what you can do for others" standard.

Here is a verse that always reminds me what type of attitude, behavior, and character I'm supposed to bring to my relationships with others: "Since God chose you to be the holy people he loves, you must clothe yourselves with tenderhearted mercy, kindness, humility, gentleness and patience" (Colossians 3:12).

If these words described you, then everyone in the world would want to be your friend, and you wouldn't worry so much about the friendship drama that seems to fill up our Facebook pages and text messages. The words in Colossians 3:12 were written to individuals who confessed a faith in Jesus Christ. I love that the scriptural author uses the word *clothe* to describe how we should display those attitudes. Mercy, kindness, humility, gentleness, and patience are supposed to be with us wherever we go, draped over our character like a favorite sweater or that perfect pair of jeans.

What gets in the way of our desire to build relationships with other women? What do you and I need to do in order to let the instructions in Colossians 3:12 shine through our lives?

WHAT A PORCUPINE CAN TEACH US

Did you know that a porcupine has thirty thousand quills on its body?[3] These sharp, pointy quills protect the creature from other animals or humans that might want to hurt it. However, those same quills also get in the way of allowing the porcupine to get close to other porcupines for warmth.

When harsh weather conditions strike, porcupines gather together in clusters to find protection from the elements. If the porcupines rushed toward one another with their quills up, it would create mass injury and likely a lot of fights. Yet a lone porcupine in harsh conditions won't survive. So what's a porcupine to do?

In order for porcupines to get close to one another, they have to lower their quills as close as possible to their skin. Only then will they be able to gather close together.

Sometimes, we can get hurt by other women. Perhaps someone gossiped about you or pretended to be your friend, but her actions and behavior inflicted wounds on your heart and soul. Other quills like envy, lies, anger, or hatred can also pierce our hearts and wound our souls. When this happens, it's tempting to cut ourselves off from making or cultivating friendships with other women in order to protect ourselves.

Yet, like the porcupine, we cannot survive alone. In fact, we were not designed to be alone. The beauty of our female heart is that it was created to love, share, nurture, and bless other women, who have lives just as complicated as our own.

THREE TYPES OF RELATIONSHIPS YOU MUST HAVE

In order to honor the principle we read about in Ecclesiastes 4:9-12, I believe there are three types of relationships that you should have in your life. These relationships serve unique purposes, and you will experience unique benefits from each:

1. Spiritual Friendships
2. Mentoring Relationships
3. "Go-To Girls"

SPIRITUAL FRIENDSHIPS

This is the kind of relationship that you have with four to six women whom you meet with at least twice a month. Some churches call these groups "small groups" or "cell groups." At our church, we call them "LifeGroups." The women in this spiritual friendship know one another and enjoy a high level of trust with one another. The purpose of your gatherings is to meet and talk about what God is doing in each of your lives. Spiritual friendships include questions like:

1. Where do you see God working in your life these days?
2. What are you celebrating in your life? Where are you struggling?
3. What are you praying about?
4. What have you read in the Bible lately that is challenging you to think or behave differently?
5. Who are you praying for and serving?
6. As you've listened to the other women share about their lives, do you think God might be leading you to think or act differently?

In this type of group, I would suggest choosing someone to lead the group and facilitate the discussion. This is the perfect format for reading discipleship-themed books with discussion questions like this book. You can also meet weekly to watch and discuss DVD-based Bible studies by a variety of best-selling Christian women Bible teachers or authors.

MENTORING RELATIONSHIPS

The idea of mentoring intimidates many people. In order to be a mentor, we feel that we have to know all of the answers, and we're afraid to admit that we don't. On the other side of the relationship, it can be embarrassing for those who need a mentor to admit how much we don't know about our faith.

Some of you are wondering what this kind of relationship looks like. Here's a framework that I hope inspires you to consider being a mentor or mentee:

1. Mentoring relationships should last more than three months but less than two years.
2. Mentor and mentee should meet at least twice a month. It is up to the mentee to contact the mentor for scheduling and confirm the appointment. (Why? Mentors

usually have very busy schedules and lack the time to
do the follow-up work.)

3. Suggested curriculum or course of study can vary based
on the area the mentee needs to work on. As always,
Scripture is a great resource for mentoring.

4. The meeting should last one to one and a half hours.
For courtesy's sake, every effort should be made to start
and end on time.

5. Important: for the initial meeting, mentor and mentee
should just try to get to know each other and determine
whether appropriate chemistry or commitment exists.
If not, this should be addressed immediately, and the
search for a new mentor should begin. However, understand that mentors and mentees do not need to become
best friends; rather, this is a concentrated period of life
during which God is invited to shape and mold each
individual.

6. The win of a mentor-mentee relationship is that both
individuals feel spiritually encouraged and challenged.
The person who is being mentored gets time, wisdom,
and encouragement from someone who's been there
and done that. Mentors benefit from the spiritual challenge of discipling someone in her faith.

GO-TO GIRLS

When tragedy strikes, you've got to have a "go-to girl." This is the
friend that knows all of your secrets and can handle all of your drama
and issues. Your go-to girl doesn't have all of the answers, but she's always there for you in a crisis, and you can trust her no matter what.

Where do you find a go-to girl? One tip: this woman is already in
your life. Think through the women whom you know the best and trust

the most. It's important to choose a go-to girl who is already a part of your life. Spend some time observing and praying about your potential go-to friendships. Since this is a critical friendship, you'll need to strategically invest time in establishing relationships with one or two go-to girls. If you aren't sure how to cultivate this type of relationship, here are some guidelines you can use:

1. Ask a few women out for a cup of coffee or lunch once or twice a month.
2. Each time, talk about your life and ask her what's going on with her life. During the conversation, you'll get a feel for the level of chemistry that you have with each other.
3. You don't need to share your deep secrets, but you do need to begin connecting at a deeper level. As you meet and connect regularly, you'll begin to talk about deeper life issues. If there is a difficult situation that arises and you feel comfortable talking about it with one of these women, then she would qualify as one of your go-to girls.

There are five women in my life whom I call my go-to girls. These women are the first ones I call when crisis hits. I know they will answer the phone whether I call or text in the middle of the night or midafternoon. And they know that I would do the same for them.

Months ago, I received such a phone call. It was 6:00 a.m. when I received a text message from one of my go-to girls. I'm not a morning person, but that weekend, I was already up. It was all in God's plan, friends. She was experiencing what I like to call a "level 10" crisis. I called her on the phone, and she answered. There were lots of tears and prayers. I didn't know what to say or do during that call. I just listened and let her know I loved her and was there for whatever she needed me to be there for.

Finding a group of these go-to friends might feel intimidating, especially if you've struggled to establish friendships. However, if you begin with intentionally developing spiritual friendships, you'll be on the right track for finding a group of go-to girls.

BEAUTY MARK
We must recognize that we need other women to encourage and challenge us to maintain our God-given beauty.

GROUP DISCUSSION QUESTIONS

1. Share one of your friendship stories. What blessed you about that relationship?

2. Think of the words in Ecclesiastes 4:9-12. Why is the woman who is alone, who doesn't have significant relationships with other women, at risk?

3. What are some of the barriers that keep women from being in close relationships with other women?

4. How do we build trust with other women?

5. What lessons do we learn from a porcupine when it comes to dealing with other women?

6. Why do we need other women to support us, especially when it comes to our ugly struggle with beauty?

PERSONAL JOURNALING QUESTIONS

1. Review Colossians 3:9-12. Which of those "best friend" qualities are you living out well? Which ones do you need to work on?

2. *What negative experiences undermine your desire to have significant friendships with other women?*

3. *Barb outlined three types of relationships that we must have as women:*

    a. *Are you involved in spiritual friendship?*

    b. *Are you involved in a mentoring relationship?*

    c. *Do you have go-to girls? Name some women with whom you can explore this type of friendship in the future?*

    d. *What do you need to do in order to cultivate these relationships in your life? What fears or barriers do you need to overcome?*

HEALING FROM THE INSIDE OUT

> *Daughter, your faith has made you well. Go in peace. Your*
> *suffering is over.*
>
> *—Mark 5:34*

It's not possible to write a book about being a woman without addressing the topic of our monthly periods. Take a deep breath, ladies. We're going in!

Who looks forward to her period each month? Although there may be times when we are concerned about an unplanned pregnancy or other hormonal issues, I've never met a woman who ran cheering through the streets proclaiming, "It's here! Seven days of joy are mine!"

Each month, we endure everything that goes along with our monthly cycle. We deal with the cramps, bleeding, maxi pads, tampons, and nervous rear glances every time we walk by a mirror during that time of the month.

For some of you, monthly menstrual cycles are a thing of the past. Whether through menopause or medical intervention, you have been freed from this part of our female experience. And I can hear you whispering "hallelujah" under your breath. But you've got daughters, sisters, and friends who are still navigating this monthly odyssey.

When I was nine years old, my mother gathered up my cousins and me to explain puberty, including our menstrual cycles. I remember the little book she had courtesy of Stayfree. The characters in the story were three young girls learning about the "wonderful changes" in their blossoming bodies. There was nothing wonderful about what my mother was reading to us. Frankly, I was horrified. And, I had questions:

> "You mean that I am going to bleed for almost seven days?"
>
> "Yes."
>
> "And this is going to happen each month?"
>
> "Yes."
>
> "*Every single month*?!"
>
> "Except for when you are pregnant and going to have a baby."
>
> "THIS IS WHERE BABIES COME FROM???!!!"

It was a traumatic afternoon. Still, I was lucky that my mom took the time to explain everything and buy me a starter kit with all types of samples in it. Many of you found out about your period when it showed up. For whatever reason, you weren't told about this developmental milestone in advance, and the only help you received once it happened was a box of sanitary napkins and a sympathetic smile.

Beautiful isn't the word we associate with our periods; we use words like *painful*, *shameful*, *inconvenient*, *embarrassing*, and even *debilitating*. Even though modern innovations like maxi pads, tampons, cups, and injections have worked to minimize the inconvenience of our menstrual cycle, many of us still feel that we are suffering each month.

Check out some of the ways that women throughout history have coped with their monthly period:[1]

- Women in ancient Greece wrapped lint around small pieces of wood for tampons. (Imagine that, ladies!)
- Ancient Roman women made tampons and pads of soft wool.
- In 1896, the first commercial sanitary pads came to market. But women weren't willing to be seen in the store purchasing them so the product failed.
- In the early twentieth century, women used baby diaper material to create homemade pads that would be pinned to undergarments.
- In the 1920s, Kotex was marketed in a unique way. These disposable pads were displayed near sales counters, and women could place money in an adjacent box so they wouldn't have to ask for the product by name.

My sisters, let's give thanks that we were born in modern times.

HER AUNT FLO DIDN'T KNOW WHEN TO GO

Almost every woman has an Aunt Flo that shows up once a month. Did you know that the average woman menstruates every twenty-eight days for approximately forty years? A normal woman will spend about 3500 days or 450 weeks of her life menstruating.

Considering how universal our menstrual cycles are to our human experience, there is a surprising sense of shame attached to our monthly periods. Do you realize that many of us spend 25 percent of our month gritting our teeth and just bearing up under our bodies? We can all agree that it's hard to connect with beauty while feeling bloated and experiencing cramps.

In Matthew 9, there was a woman who had been bleeding for twelve years. She approached Jesus and the disciples as they traveled to the home of a religious leader whose daughter had just died. Matthew

9:20-22 records the short version of this story: "Just then a woman who had suffered for twelve years with constant bleeding came up behind him. She touched the fringe of his robe, for she thought, 'If I can just touch his robe, I will be healed.' Jesus turned around, and when he saw her he said, 'Daughter, be encouraged! Your faith has made you well.' And the woman was healed at that moment."

Imagine your period lasting twelve years without stopping! If you've suffered from fibroid tumors or other maladies, you know the frustration of going for four to eight weeks with daily bleeding, but what about every day for twelve years? That's almost 4,400 days in a row—more than a lifetime's worth for a normal healthy woman. Some of us would be looking for the nearest bridge to jump off of, right?

Notice the word *suffering*. A longer version of this woman's story is recorded in Mark 5. Although he doesn't record her name, Mark mentions that this woman spent everything she had looking for healing. Mark also reports that the woman suffered at the hand of many physicians while looking for healing, and instead of getting better, her condition worsened.

How bad could it have been for her? The pain was more than physical; everything about this woman's life was painful:

- Under the religious laws of the time, menstruating women were considered unclean so she would have separated from her household and community. Most women endured this for the normal seven days; but after a few years, this woman probably lost her husband and family because she wouldn't have been permitted to fulfill her role as a wife and mother.
- Some translations use the word *hemorrhage* when describing the issue of blood. She likely soaked through her ancient menstrual padding hourly.

- The doctors of the time would have subjected her to painful, inhumane experimental treatments to try to eliminate the flow, and knowing how desperate she was, those doctors would have charged a large sum.
- Due to the substantial loss of blood, the woman probably had anemia. This meant she would have been weak, frail, and vulnerable during all of those years.[2]

For any woman who has endured painful monthly cycles, it wouldn't take much to visualize the emotional and physical pain of the woman. We don't know her name, but we know what it feels like to lie on the couch rolled in a ball or to lie in a dark room with a menstrual-induced migraine. But we don't know the pain of being separated from our family or community because of something that is supposed to be natural but seems to be out of control.

So, what's a woman to do?

DESPERATE TIMES CALL FOR DESPERATE MEASURES

Then there was the day when the woman saw Jesus walking along the road. She didn't know the Jesus that we know. We know about Jesus' faithfulness and sacrifice so that we can have a relationship with him. This woman didn't know those things. She only knew the stories of what people were saying about him. She heard that Jesus raised people from the dead and healed people from their diseases. No doubt she wondered if Jesus could help her.

What made that woman reach out for Jesus that day? In her weak condition, it might have seemed too difficult to think about fighting the crowd to get to Jesus. But she did. Why? In a word: desperation. According to the religious laws of the time, she shouldn't have even been out in that crowd because she was considered unclean. I can't help but imagine that every morning when this woman woke up, she prayed that God would heal her. And, after enduring each painful day, she would curl up in a ball and cry out the same prayer again.

Can you relate to her? Maybe you aren't praying for relief from a difficult menstrual cycle, but maybe you are praying for a pregnancy that won't come or freedom from the memory of rape or abuse. Maybe you are praying for God to send your dream man your way. Whatever the pain or whatever the prayer, each day, you petition God in hope or desperation. Each day, it seems like an answer will never come. In the meantime, you, too, feel like you are bleeding out.

In Mark's account, we learn that a crowd had gathered around Jesus on his way to the religious leader's home. No doubt these people had needs and believed that Jesus could come to their rescue. Each person wanted Jesus to hear his or her story in hopes that he would grant his or her need.

Not this woman. She wasn't aiming to talk to Jesus. She just wanted to touch him. When I close my eyes, I can see that tired, weak woman pressing her way through the crowd, elbows banging into her translucent skin. I can see her grimace and the tears rolling down her face from the pain of bodies jostling against hers.

Yet she pressed on toward Christ with the following hope: *If I can just touch his robe, I will be healed.*

Her fingers stretch forward. *Just a little more.* She closes her eyes and leans forward a little more. *Almost there.* Her fingers flutter in the air until she feels the rough cloth of Jesus' robe. In that moment of first contact, I can hear her breathless whisper, *I know you can heal me.*

Contact. Scriptures tells us that in that moment, her bleeding stopped, and she knew that she was free from suffering. I wonder if her body tingled or if she experienced a jolt. All we know is that she was healed from the inside out. Not only was her physical body healed, but that healing opened other opportunities. The woman could now dream of rejoining her family and community.

While the crowd pressed and grabbed at Jesus—and no doubt many people were touching his person—Mark tells us that Jesus turned and asked the question: "Who touched my robe?"

Jesus already knew the woman touched his robe. Under Jewish law, he could have chastised her for touching him while she was unclean. Instead, Jesus gave her an opportunity to testify to what just happened in her life. The woman came to Jesus, fell to her knees, and told Jesus what happened.

I don't know about you, but I would be a babbling mess in that moment. She would not only be terrified that she had offended Jesus but also struggle to find the right words to express her thanks and gratitude.

When Jesus speaks again, his first word is "Daughter." That tells us all that we need to know about how Jesus feels about the woman. Jesus only uses such terms as *son* and *daughter* when referring to believers. As a result of her faith, this woman was now a part of Jesus' family.

GO IN PEACE

Jesus' next statement to the woman is very powerful: "Go in peace." The word for *peace* is *shalom*. In this context, *shalom* speaks of wholeness, well-being, prosperity, security, friendship, and salvation entering into her life. There's something so beautiful about each of those words. Each of these elements was missing in the woman's life before she dared to grab Jesus' cloak. Yet, in that moment of great faith, she was rewarded with everything she'd lost over the years.

Peace is a beautiful thing, isn't it? Peace is living free from strife or worry. Peace is an inward calm that flows out through our facial expressions, attitude, and behaviors. Even when our solutions seem limited or our circumstances seem hopeless, peace can get us through to the other side.

When the woman left the crowd that day, she must have run back to her community to tell them what had happened. Not only that, but her heart and mind were free to dream of what her life could become. She had a chance to live and love. She could kiss and hug her loved ones after years of isolation. She had the freedom to throw her head back and laugh without heartache. Peace.

Do you need that kind of peace? If so, Jesus invites you to come near him, too.

REACHING OUT TO JESUS

Ladies, none us escape this life without wounds. Some of us have been hurt so deeply that we feel as if we are hemorrhaging our lifeblood with no end in sight. Like the woman in the Bible, some of you are drained from the circumstances of your life. Day after day, you drag yourself out of bed. You manage to survive the day just so that you can collapse back on your bed at night. Drawing your knees up to your chest, you weep. You cry out morning after morning for God to stop the bleeding, and at the end of each day, you repeat that prayer again.

In these moments, you don't want to think about beauty. You can't even see beauty, because ugly feels like it is suffocating you to death. Since you can't see beauty, then it's only natural that you see shame. Even if the hemorrhaging isn't your fault, you still feel ashamed of that memory and the fact that you can't find healing, no matter how hard you try.

I don't know what situation, circumstance, or life event feels like it is draining the life from you, but I do know this: you must reach out to Jesus. And you can't let anything get in the way of reaching out to him: "This High Priest of ours understands our weaknesses, for he faced all of the same testings we do, yet he did not sin. So let us come boldly to the throne of our gracious God. There we will receive his mercy, and we will find grace to help us when we need it most" (Hebrews 4:15-16).

Jesus knows what it feels like to bleed physically and emotionally from every pore in your body. If you've been in church, you may have heard the pastor say, "Jesus bled for you." Did you realize that this isn't just a metaphor? It's true.

Richard Swenson, MD, author of *More Than Meets the Eye*, calculates that when Jesus was beaten and crucified, the number of blood cells contained within the volume of blood he lost equals at least one cell for every person who lived before or since Jesus walked this earth. Jesus bled so that each and every one of us could experience healing, not just for eternity, but on earth as well.[3]

We must reach out to Jesus. We must reach toward him like the woman. I know you may be weak. You may be tired. You might have tried to find an answer to the pain you've suffered through a lot of different remedies, but have you reached out to Jesus? What's stopping you?

Yes, if you are physically suffering, for goodness' sake, go to the doctor. If you have been emotionally hemorrhaging from a traumatic event, get thee to the therapist or psychiatrist without delay. But don't forget to reach out for Jesus.

Just what kind of peace does Jesus bring? In John 16:33, Jesus is talking about the times in life when we will suffer. In this passage, Jesus tells us that even in those moments, we can have *shalom*, or peace: "I have told you all this so that you may have peace in me. Here on earth you will have many trials and sorrows. But take heart, because I have overcome the world."

My dear friend, wherever you are bleeding right now, Jesus can bring you peace. He can restore you to wholeness and well-being. Come to him—and don't let anything stop you.

If you aren't sure what to say, here is how you can start:

> Dear Jesus, I am drained from life. I am hemorrhaging
> from the pain of _____, and I don't know if I

can make it another day. Jesus, I am coming to you like the woman in Matthew. I'm reaching out for you. I need the peace that you promised. Bless me with shalom. Bless me with wholeness and well-being. Give me peace. Amen.

Pray this prayer for as long as you need to. Pray it when you feel like your peace is slipping away. If you have peace, then pray this prayer for the family and friends in your life who need to experience Jesus' peace. *Shalom,* my sisters.

BEAUTY MARK
Come boldly to Jesus. He will give you peace.
He won't let you down.

GROUP DISCUSSION QUESTIONS

1. How do you feel about your monthly period? What are (or were) some of the words you use to describe it?

2. Why is there a sense of embarrassment or shame attached to our monthly periods?

3. What do you think of the ancient forms of feminine hygiene products? How must it have felt to be a woman born before our modern times? How has medical and manufacturing progress blessed us?

4. Discuss the story of the woman with the issue of blood. What stands out to you about her story or her interaction with Jesus?

5. How is the peace that Jesus brings us so different than the peace we try to gain on our own?

6. How can the ladies in your group pray for you to experience Jesus' shalom or peace?

PERSONAL JOURNALING QUESTIONS

1. How did you find out about your monthly period? Did you sense shame or embarrassment related to this part of your female experience?

2. How does your life relate to the woman with the issue of blood?

3. Is there a circumstance or past event that causes you to feel like you are hemorrhaging? Describe how the pain feels. How does it drain you? What are the prayers you offer to God?

4. Finish this statement: "For me to have peace in this area of my life, _____ needs to happen."

5. When Jesus says that he wants to give you shalom or peace, this means that he wants to restore your sense of wholeness or well-being. What would your life look like if you allowed Jesus to bring shalom in your life? Describe how you would feel or behave.

6. What do you need to do in order to allow Jesus to bring peace to you? What attitude, beliefs, or behaviors do you need to surrender to his throne so that you can receive the mercy and peace he promises?

IF THE BARN NEEDS PAINTIN'

For everything there is a season, a time for every activity under heaven.

—*Ecclesiastes 3:1*

Once I attended a conference, and the speaker on the podium looked at all of the women in the crowd while talking about being a woman and announced the following: "Ladies, if the barn needs painting, then paint it!"

The audience of women cheered. Meanwhile, I'm thinking, "What barn?"

What she meant was that it is OK to take care of the things that need to be taken care of. It's OK to take care of our bodies. It's OK to take time for ourselves. We have the freedom to embrace beautiful things as well as the encouragement to cultivate inner beauty.

My husband's family lives in the rural northwestern part of Ohio, so when we drive out to visit his family, we pass dozens of barns along the way. We see big barns, small barns, and every size in between. I love classic red barns. These large structures with bold colors and simple lines remind me of some of my favorite childhood books, such as *Charlotte's Web* and the *Little House* books. Those barns were as much a part of the story as the family that lived across the yard in the house.

My heart saddens at the sight of old, dilapidated barns. Once upon a time that barn was new and glorious. I imagine the proud farmer and his wife standing in front of that barn that they sacrificed to build. I see a tear in the farmer's eye as he saw that barn as security for his family's future. That new barn would hold their precious livestock and keep their harvest dry. That barn represented the hopes and dreams of generations.

The farmer and his wife never imagined a day when that barn would start to deteriorate. Perhaps money was tight, so the farmer couldn't replace busted wood planks or patch the roof. At some point, however, I'm sure that the farmer realized that his barn was starting to look tired and worn. I'm also sure of this: that he spent years quietly promising himself the same thing over and over again: *I'll take care of it one of these days.*

Unfortunately, that day never came.

How often have you put off caring for yourself, believing that once you took care of everything for everyone else, then you could do something for yourself? How many times have you said, "Oh! I would *love* to do that. Someday."

Someday, I'll have lunch with _____.
Someday, I'll take up a hobby.
Someday, I'll work out regularly.
Someday, I'll update my haircut.
Someday, I'll take a vacation.

What's your "someday"?

I have a gift certificate for a free massage at my friend's spa. I love getting massages, but for the past six months, this gift certificate has been sitting in my purse because I can't figure out how and when to use it. It should be easy. I should just pick up the phone and schedule an appointment. But I don't. Well, I won't. Um, I can't.

In my mind, for me to enjoy myself or do something for myself, first, I have to finish the invisible checklist of all of the things that I need to accomplish as a wife, mother, and employee. I've convinced myself that until every single need of every person I care about at home or work is taken care of, I can't punch the clock to care for myself.

When I think back to those dilapidated barns, I know the farmer never foresaw such a fate. On the day the barn was finished, he didn't say, "Well, one day this barn will be missing half a roof and lean to one side." So, what was the tipping point? Was there a day that suddenly changed everything, or was the barn's sad state the result of a slow, barely noticeable neglect? Perhaps that farmer just kept saying, "Someday."

WHY WE WON'T LET "SOMEDAY" BECOME "NOW"?

As I mentioned, I have a spa gift certificate in my purse. I'm going to have to force myself to make that appointment even though so many different areas of my life are incomplete. I need to deal with an insurance claim for ice damage to our dining room and file paperwork for a health insurance reimbursement. The dogs need their heartworm medicine, and I need to write checks for the girls' upcoming school trip. Oh, and yes, I need to reschedule that mammogram. Again.

For some reason, I believe that I can't use that gift certificate until all of those items are taken care of. It's crazy but true. And there is one word that describes the feeling behind my procrastination of this good thing: *guilt*.

If I do something for myself before everything else is taken care of, then I will feel guilty. My definition of guilt is "failing to living up to expectations."

Most of us are pros when it comes to feeling guilty. What are we feeling guilty about? Here's the short list:

We feel guilty for not being perfect.

We feel guilty about being fat.

We feel guilty about how we look.

We feel guilty that we might care too much about how we look.

We feel guilty about working too much.

We feel guilty about not having enough time to help others.

We feel guilty helping those who should be helping themselves.

We feel guilty when we don't call.

We feel guilty about feeling guilty.

As women, we understand guilt. In fact, some of us have been feeling guilty so long, it's like that worn-out sweater in your drawer. You pull it out and put it on because it's what you know and it feels comfy even though it doesn't do anything positive for your figure. Yes, some of us are very comfortable with feeling guilty. It's our default emotion.

What do we feel guilty about? Often our lives do not match up to our expectations. In our minds, there is this perfect person that we want to be. When we do not match up to this ideal, then even our best effort seems worthless.

I can wake up early, work out, make my kids breakfast, get to work on time, perform well throughout the day, and say only nice things to my husband that evening, but if I burn dinner, I might let myself believe that the entire day is a failure. When I look at myself in the mirror that night, I look into the face of failure. If I'm not careful, I start to believe that unless I performed flawlessly all day long, I do not deserve to do anything good for myself.

Dr. Brené Brown defines guilt as: "I've done something bad."[1] When we miss expectations, we might believe that we've done bad, and people who are bad deserve to be punished. So is it possible that when we fail to live up to the perfect image of ourselves, we punish ourselves by not taking care of us? Do you inwardly whisper the words, "But, I don't deserve to . . ."?

What expectations do you have for yourself? Which of those expectations causes you to feel guilt?

> I cannot rest until everything I need to do is done.
> I expect for my home to be spotless, Pinterest-organized, and clean.
> I expect to finish my to-do list by the end of each day.
> I expect that I will fulfill any reasonable request that important people in my life ask of me.
> I expect _____.

When it comes to caring for ourselves, guilt will impede or arrest our good intentions. As long as there is someone else in our life to care for, we will put ourselves at the back of the line. Friends, when will we understand that caring for ourselves and caring for others are not mutually exclusive? If we can multitask other areas of our lives, surely we can figure this out. We don't have to abandon our obligations or those whom we love in order to take care of ourselves. And we don't have to feel guilty about it either.

How do we reset the expectations of our lives so that we can live in freedom rather than in guilt?

HONORING THE RHYTHM OF LIFE

King Solomon reigned from around 970 BC to 930 BC. Known as the wisest man who ever lived, Solomon had unmatched brilliance. Yet he entered the final years of his reign disillusioned by all he had known. Written in 935 BC, Ecclesiastes records some of the lessons that Solomon learned. Read the following aloud from Ecclesiastes 3:1-11:

For everything there is a season,
a time for every activity under heaven.
A time to be born and a time to die.
A time to plant and a time to harvest.
A time to kill and a time to heal.
A time to tear down and a time to build up.
A time to cry and a time to laugh,
A time to grieve and a time to dance.
A time to scatter stones and a time to gather stones.
A time to embrace and a time to turn away.
A time to search and a time to quit searching.
A time to keep and a time to throw away.
A time to tear and a time to mend.
A time to be quiet and a time to speak.
A time to love and a time to hate.
A time for war and a time for peace.

What do people really get for all their hard work? I have
seen the burden God has placed on us all. Yet God has
made everything beautiful for its own time. He has planted
eternity in the human heart, but even so, people cannot
see the whole scope of God's work from beginning to end.

Which of those experiences have occurred in your life in the past
year? Have you made time to cry and laugh? Have you had the time to
be quiet and to speak up?

There are many things that I love about this section of Scripture. Notice that there is a God-ordained rhythm to our lives. Each experience
weaves into the next. Furthermore, there are some things that we cannot do "for now" but that won't last "forever." When I talk to women, I
frequently reassure them, "Honey, this is your 'for now' life. But it won't
be forever, just for now." We progress through so many different peri-

ods of life, so our expectations of what we can do and achieve should change depending on the phase of life we are living in.

There are some things in life that are just too hard to do right now, but years from now, you'll accomplish them with no problem. However, you've got to pay attention to the condition of your emotional, physical, and spiritual selves so that you know when the paint is starting to chip in your heart, body, or soul. Don't wait until you're leaning to the side before you try to fix one of these areas. Better to patch and repaint repeatedly in small sections than to have to do it all at once.

ASK THIS QUESTION

What do Solomon's words have to do with escaping the guilt that pervades our lives? When we recognize that there is a time and place for everything, then we are free to care for ourselves without bearing the guilt or burden that someone else is suffering.

There is a wonderful question that Dr. Henry Cloud and Dr. John Townsend ask in their prolific best seller, *Boundaries*.[2] If you are struggling with guilt, especially as it relates to your relationships, you probably need to drop my book and go get theirs. (I probably shouldn't say that, but I mean it.)

Here is their question when trying to decide whether or not it is appropriate to allocate time or energy toward someone or something: *Is this time or money or energy well spent?*[3]

Suppose you are a single mom raising three boys and your ex-husband isn't always great about paying child support. Although you work to make ends meet, you struggle to pay for your boys' extracurricular activities. Once a month or so, a friend invites you out to dinner at Chili's, hardly a high-end restaurant. You've reluctantly gone along for months, but you feel guilty for spending a night away and spending precious money, even though the boys are with their dad. I want you to think about that question: *Is this time or money or energy well spent?*

If it is a good friend, who blesses you, then the answer is yes! The time away nurturing a friendship as well as the opportunity to relax and laugh come at a nominal cost.

What if you love wearing makeup and buying clothes? How would you answer that question: *Is this time or money or energy well spent?* The answer is, it depends. It depends on where you are shopping, why you are shopping, how much you spend, and how much you can afford to spend. If you are shopping because you enjoy it but aren't defined by your clothes and you can afford what you are buying, then have fun! However, if shopping is the way that you satisfy some other hunger in your life, such as replacing acceptance or love, then no, that time, money, or energy isn't well spent.

DO YOU NEED TO PAINT THE BARN?

Is there a place in your life that has been neglected because you've been feeling guilty about other things? You don't have to feel guilty any longer! No matter your season of life, you can take time away for yourself without feeling selfish. Don't wait any longer to deal with the hurting, damaged, or broken areas of your life!

The Discussion and Personal Journaling Questions at the end of this chapter can help you figure out where you need to devote some time and attention to yourself. Furthermore, you should be honest with yourself about the situations that create guilt and use some of the practical suggestions posed in this chapter to free yourself from guilt.

BEAUTY MARK
Make it a priority to take care of the areas of your life that are threatening your future.

GROUP DISCUSSION QUESTIONS

1. Barb uses barns as a metaphor for how we care for ourselves. How's your barn looking lately?

2. Are there any areas of your life—emotional, physical, spiritual, financial, or relational—that you've been neglecting?

3. What are some of the most common excuses you give for not taking better care of yourself?

4. What makes you feel guilty? How often do you feel guilty because you haven't lived up to your own expectations?

5. Ecclesiastes 3:1-11 outlines a God-ordained rhythm of life. Which experiences have you had in the past year?

6. What are some things in life that you can or can't do "for now," but those changes won't last "forever"?

7. What did you think of Drs. Cloud and Townsend's question: Is this time or money or energy well spent? Name some times when you can ask yourself that question? How might it help you alleviate some guilt?

PERSONAL JOURNALING QUESTIONS

1. What are you celebrating in your life right now?

2. What are you struggling with in your life right now?

3. If you cannot answer either of these questions, what are some of the reasons?

4. What expectations need to be realigned in order to deal with guilt overtaking the time needed to care for yourself?

5. Where do you need to find time to "paint the barn" in your life before more substantial damage takes place?

BECOMING A WOMAN WHO C.A.R.E.S.

Don't you realize that your body is the temple of the Holy Spirit,
who lives in you and was given to you by God? You do not belong
to yourself, for God bought you with a high price. So you must
honor God with your body.

—*1 Corinthians 6:19-20*

Throughout our journey together, we've invested a lot of time and effort into understanding our ugly struggle with beauty, defining divine beauty, practicing techniques that will allow us to see God first over our flaws, and reframing certain areas of our feminine physique that we normally wouldn't identify as beautiful. We've also identified the characteristics of inner beauty and learned that God desires to cultivate this kind of precious beauty in each of our lives. In the last few chapters, we've uncovered certain threats that can undermine or hijack our pursuit of inner beauty.

Just take a moment and breathe. Seriously, take a deep cleansing breath. *How are you doing, my friend? How's your day going?* If you've made it this far into our journey, just know that you've been an answer to my prayer. Yes, I've been praying for you. I may not know your name, but I do know this: you are beautiful. You've always been beautiful, but you might not have truly believed it. Hopefully, you believe it now.

Lots of books address weight loss, exercise, style, and makeup. Although I'm going to share a few of my thoughts on each of those topics, the majority of our discussion will unpack the answer to why we need to become a woman who C.A.R.E.S.

WHAT IS A WOMAN WHO C.A.R.E.S.?

Since physical beauty is such a broad topic, I wanted to create a context that would not only guide our discussion but also provide a framework that you could use in the future as a kind of checklist for yourself. Here is what C.A.R.E.S. stands for: Clothing, Appetite, Rest, Exercise, and Smile.

CLOTHING

I know that about half of those reading this chapter hate shopping. Another large percentage of you hates how your body looks in your current wardrobe. I am amazed at how many pairs of yoga pants appear at the grocery store and the mall. Not that many women do yoga! Some of our ugly struggles with beauty have been so discouraging that we would rather tug on a pair of sweats or yoga pants than look in a closet full of clothes that won't make us look any better than we look right now.

It's OK to look and feel good, especially if you have worked to cultivate a godly, gentle, and quiet spirit. Since you've committed yourself to developing inner beauty, you should want to care about how you present your physical body.

I've also discovered that when my clothes look good on me, I feel good and am more likely to reach out and be motivated to connect with others. When we don't feel like we look good, we are less likely to reach out to love or serve others.

One of the best things I ever did for myself was to promise myself three things:

1. I would only purchase clothing or shoes that I absolutely, positively *loved*.
2. I would only purchase items that looked great on me. Not good, but *great*.
3. If something didn't fit, I would get rid of it.

Ladies, I've lived by these three rules for many years, and they are the only three rules that I have for shopping. Consequently, my closet is much smaller than most people would think. But I love everything in my closet, and when I don't love something anymore or it doesn't fit, I get rid of it.

I've had to make peace with the reality that there are some styles and stores that don't work for me. Yes, I enjoy great sales and bargains, but too many of our closets are filled with clothes we purchased for the wrong reasons, like because it was on clearance or because it looked good on someone else.

For many years, I watched Clinton and Stacy on the long-running show *What Not to Wear*. This show helped me determine what type of clothing and which styles were right for not only my body but also my personality. I watched as women of all shapes, sizes, and ages tried on clothing and accessories. Clinton and Stacy provided a world-class education on which kinds of fabrics and cuts were best for each kind of body shape.

I wear jeans every day. I learned that based on my body type, I would look best in tall-length, low-rise, boot-cut, dark denim jeans. I found stores that sold specifically those kind of jeans, and sure enough, when I tried them on, I looked and felt great! At times, I would try to wear other kinds of jeans, such as mid-rise or a stone wash. I looked OK, but I didn't look or feel as great as I did in the ones that were really right for me.

Some of you feel intimidated or overwhelmed at the time and effort it will take to discover what is right for you. Yes, it will take an investment of time. However, you'll end up saving hundreds of hours of frustration at the store or in your closet in the future. Once you know what you look great in, you won't waste time or money buying things that make you less than beautiful.

Practical Tips

1. Try on everything in your closet. Everything.
2. Divide your clothes, shoes, and accessories into in two piles: things you love that look great on you and everything else.
3. Get rid of everything else. Just trust me. You won't be left naked. Let the other pile go. It's a good idea to invite a friend over to help you through this process.

APPETITE

If we are what we eat, then what does your food say about you? We know that we are supposed to eat more vegetables than junk food. We also know that water is better for us than pop or soda. So, why don't we do the things we are supposed to do?

We lack conviction. We've got a lot of head knowledge about what's right, but our hearts just aren't into it. We don't *feel* like it, right? Each one of us has a hunger, and we will satisfy our hunger based on our convictions.

Years ago, I heard pastor and best-selling author Andy Stanley give a talk titled "What's Your Bowl of Stew?"[1] He shared the story of how Jacob's brother, Esau, succumbed to an out-of-control hunger and lost his blessing in favor of a bowl of stew. Andy warns us that if we aren't aware of our appetites, we will miss out on many blessings because we will fill our bodies and our lives with food or things that will never satisfy us.

Women are notorious emotional eaters. We hunger for stability, healing, peace, or love. When our hunger for those things goes unsatisfied, we find satisfaction in other ways, often food.

Here are a few questions:

1. On a scale of 1 (never) to 10 (always), how often do you eat when you feel badly about yourself or your situation?
2. What kinds of foods do you pick up but have difficulty putting down?
3. What kind of emotional, relational, social, or financial voids are you experiencing right now?

If we are going to be women who care about our bodies, then we need to care what we put into our bodies. I'm not talking about organic food or vegan diets. I'm talking about understanding the heart issues behind our food consumption. My friends, food should not be a substitute cure for pain or emptiness in other areas of our lives.

Practical Tips

1. Even if you aren't an emotional eater, keep track of what you eat over the next week. You can use apps like SparkPeople to log your consumption electronically. Sometimes, it's just good to assess how well you are or aren't nourishing your body.
2. There are some food-related issues that you may not be able to uncover or evaluate on your own, especially if your out-of-control appetite stems from abuse, shame, or other issues. Love yourself enough to ask for help.
3. One of the best studies on this topic is *Made to Crave* by Lysa TerKeurst.[2]

REST

Friends, the pace of our lives is exhausting—and we're exhausted. Thanks to technology and innovation, our complex world has created more complexity for our lives. Since we can do more, we do more. My iPhone never leaves my side. It allows me to talk, text, send e-mail, shop, schedule, purchase, play, and watch every single minute of every single hour of each day.

When was the last time that you completely disconnected from your life and did absolutely nothing? I mean nothing. Folding laundry while watching television doesn't count. Neither does paying bills on your iPad in bed.

I'm talking about rest. When was the last time you rested? If you've forgotten the definition of *rest*, it is when we cease from all labor. Rest happens when we stop performing tasks and disengage our minds from thinking about those tasks. Let me ask you again: when was the last time you rested?

I'm not good at resting. I'm so bad at it that anyone who knows me is laughing aloud right now. I think some of you are bad at it, too. Why? We are always taking care of someone or something. It doesn't matter if we are single, married, or single again, our feminine mind-set drives us to constantly nurture whatever environment we are in, whether motivating our staff to generate more sales, growing our garden, raising our children, or caring for our homes.

At some point, we've got to shut ourselves down. Friends, we can't give what we don't have, and even when we run ourselves into the ground for good reasons, we're still run down.

It's time to rest.

I love that God blesses rest in Genesis 2:2-3: "On the seventh day God had finished his work of creation, so he rested from all his work. And God blessed the seventh day and declared it holy, because it was the day when he rested from all his work of creation."

Here is how God models rest for us:

1. God prioritized what He needed to do.
2. When God's work was finished, He stopped and didn't add anything else to it.

3. There was one day that God set apart from the other days in order to rest.

The Jewish word we use to describe the kind of rest God models for us is *Sabbath*. During Sabbath rest, we cease our labor. So, if you are employed, you'll need to establish your Sabbath on your day off. If you work seven days a week, you'll need to rethink your job. Why would I make such a bold statement? When we rest, we turn the care and custody of our lives into God's hands for Him to protect and provide while we rejuvenate. I understand that there may be certain periods of life when we work more than usual, but this should not be your rhythm of life.

I love Fridays! I work about six days a week, but not on Friday. Thursday nights are exciting for me because I know Friday's up next. My toughest challenge is shutting down my brain from thinking about work. So, I read fiction books and eat grocery store sushi in bed. I take long walks and practice deep breathing. I sit and pray. Sometimes, I just wander around my house in the quiet. By the end of each Sabbath rest, my soul is refreshed, and I feel alive again.

Practical Tips

1. When you choose your day of rest, keep it consistent.
2. Do not schedule anything on that day. It's not rest if you've got a schedule.
3. What about mothers with children or women caring for elderly loved ones? God still wants you to experience rest. This means that you might need to get creative with solutions such as trading babysitting or even paying for respite care. Trust me, any expense or effort you put into arranging for your Sabbath rest will have an incredible ROI (return on investment)!

EXERCISE

Like the topic of food, much has been written about exercise. I'm not a fitness expert, so we're not going to talk about what kinds of exercise are best for you. What we will talk about is why we should care about developing strong, fit bodies.

Ephesians 2:10 contains the answer to why it matters if our bodies are physically fit: "For we are God's masterpiece. He has created us anew in Christ Jesus, so we can do the good things he planned for us long ago."

God has plans for us to make an impact in this world. If His plan is for the gospel message to be shared around the world, and He commands us to share that message, then our bodies have to be prepared to carry out that work. Yes, we've got technology, but the gospel is highly relational. In order to serve others, we must be fit to serve them in a way that fulfills their needs.

I love going on mission trips! I've been on numerous overseas trips; and whether I'm building a house or speaking at women's conferences, I realize that my stamina is connected to my overall level of fitness. In order to serve the needs of others, I must be fit enough to address those needs. In fact, I tend to increase my workouts before going on missions trips to make sure that I am as fit and healthy as I can be.

Some of you want to volunteer more, but your bodies can't keep up. The Apostle Paul tells us that physical fitness does have value—granted, it isn't as valuable as spiritual fitness, but it is important.

I think that Christian women can improve greatly in this area. We've created too many excuses for why we aren't fit. Could our lack of commitment eventually lead to our lack of impact? How can we be beacons of light in a dark world when we run out of breath after fifteen minutes? How can we go into the highways and byways to tell the world about Christ when our bodies are weak from sedentary lives?

Practical Tips

1. Move your body every day. Walk somewhere each day. Don't worry about how fast you walk; just walk.
2. You'll be more successful in staying committed to getting fit or working out if you have a friend doing it with you.
3. Set a God-sized goal for fitness. Tie your fitness goal to something that will impact the kingdom of God.

SMILE

Where's your smile? Since we care about so many things, our hearts can become overburdened on a regular basis. Those burdens bury our beautiful smiles!

Just as the eyes are said to be the windows to the soul, a smile can be the portal to our hearts. Our smile should be a reflection of our quiet spirit and tranquility. We can be concerned about certain circumstances, but our hearts should not be gripped with worry. Stress and worry will diminish our physical beauty.

Stand in the mirror and smile at yourself. Notice how your eyes and cheeks lift. Pay attention to how your white teeth add a subtle glow to the rest of your face. Remember that smiling not only improves your mood but also uses fewer wrinkle-causing muscles.

Yes, there are some women who hide behind fake smiles. There is something to be said for "fake it, 'til you make it," especially if you're smiling through a temporarily difficult situation. However, if your smile always feels or looks fake, consider rereading chapter twelve's content on inner beauty and revisit the qualities you'll want to work toward.

Practical Tips

1. Whenever you look into a mirror, smile at yourself. You deserve to experience the beauty of your own smile.

2. Maintaining an attitude of gratitude is a guaranteed smile builder. Whether you write out a daily list or mentally keep track, make sure to list everything in your life that blesses you on a regular basis.

3. Smile at everyone you see. Trust me, you'll bless untold multitudes of people in this way.

Understanding the reasons *why* you need to be a woman who C.A.R.E.S. is the most important motivation for becoming one.

GROUP DISCUSSION QUESTIONS

1. When you think about becoming a woman who C.A.R.E.S., which area(s) create(s) the most tension for you?

2. Why do many Christian women give themselves a pass on healthy eating or working out?

3. If you had to choose one area to work on this week, which area would it be? What would success look like for you in that area?

4. As a group, share some other practical tips with one another that may not have been mentioned.

PERSONAL JOURNALING QUESTIONS

1. How well do you care for your body? What are you doing well? Where do you need to improve?

2. What physical issues are holding you back right now? Have you identified the reason why?

3. Commitment is important to making real changes. In what areas do you think God is calling you to a new commitment? What will be the steps in keeping that commitment?

BALANCING INNER
AND PHYSICAL BEAUTY

She is clothed with strength and dignity, and she laughs without
fear of the future. When she speaks, her words are wise, and she
gives instructions with kindness.

—*Proverbs 31:25-26*

In June 2013, millions of people around the world watched as American daredevil Nik Wallenda became the first man to walk on a tightrope across an expanse near the Grand Canyon.[1] Unharnessed atop a wire stretched over a quarter of a mile 1,500 feet in the air, Wallenda traversed the canyon, stopping twice when winds exceeding thirty miles per hour made it difficult for him to continue his death-defying stunt. Millions listened as Wallenda prayed without ceasing almost every step of the way until he reached the other side of the canyon safely. I don't remember breathing the entire twenty-two minutes of his terror-inducing feat.

Understanding the importance of balance was the main key to Wallenda's successful walk across that great divide. There were some variables that he couldn't control, such as the strength of the wind gusts or how much the wire moved. As we listened to Wallenda's audio, he didn't waste time or energy griping about things he couldn't do anything about. His focus remained fixated on what he could control, such as his mind-set, his pace, and most important, how he shifted his weight as he crossed the great divide.

Nik Wallenda's story is a metaphor for our lives. There will always be situations and circumstances outside of our control. Yet, when we learn how to live in balance, particularly when we learn how to shift our weight in response to uncontrollable factors, we can make forward progress toward where we want to be in life.

Balance doesn't only mean maintaining an equal weight on each side. Balance can also be achieved when different elements are in correct proportions.

Cooking provides a great example of this concept. When cooking, it is important to make sure that flavors are balanced even though the amounts may not be in equal proportions. Some flavors are more potent than others, so mixing them in equal amounts will not have the desired effect. Pure vanilla added in small amounts magnifies the yummy factor of most cookies or cakes. However, if a cake recipe calls for a half-cup of milk and one tablespoon of vanilla, I would ruin the recipe if I added a half-cup of vanilla just so that it could be the same amount as the milk. There are times in life when balance doesn't mean equality, but rather proportionality.

PICTURING THE BALANCE

We've spent a lot of time and effort diagnosing our ugly struggle with beauty and equipping ourselves to push back against the things that stop our inner beauty from flourishing. We've also equipped ourselves to understand the practical applications of both inner and physical beauty. Now, it is time for us to put it all together according to the correct proportions. So, what does that look like? I'm a visual person, so I wanted to create a picture of what beauty should look like. Furthermore, I wanted to create a visual that you could use in order to explain God's design for beautiful women when talking to your friends who may not have read *Enough Already*. So, this is what a picture of balanced inner and physical beauty could look like:

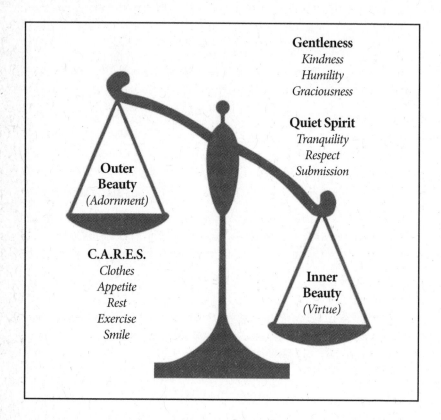

A few things should stand out as you look at this diagram. Notice that inner beauty is lower than outer beauty. Remember, this is a scale, so heavier features hang lower than lighter features. Therefore, since inner beauty should be emphasized more than physical beauty, it has greater weight. Additionally, the qualities of inner and physical beauty are listed with the scales.

This visual graphic reinforces the idea that both types of beauty have their place, as long as we cultivate them in the right balance.

Now, we're going to look at the story of my favorite woman in the Bible. Esther demonstrates what happens when a woman leverages her inner and physical beauty in correct proportion, and in doing so, she is able to save the lives of her people.

ESTHER: A BALANCED BEAUTY

Once upon a time there was a Jewish man named Mordecai. He lived in Persia and worked as a scribe for King Ahasuerus (Xerxes), the king of Persia. Generations before, the Jewish people lost their homeland and many, like Mordecai, were living in Persia. At some point in time, Mordecai took in his cousin, a young orphan girl. This is how Esther 2:7 describes the young girl: "This man had a very beautiful and lovely young cousin, Hadassah, who was also called Esther."

Esther is my favorite figure in the Bible. Her attitude, beliefs, and character demonstrate the ideal balance of inner and physical beauty. The snapshot of her life story rests about halfway through the Old Testament.

If you are not familiar with the Bible, the book of Esther contains a unique feature: it's the only book in the Bible in which God's name isn't mentioned. Within the ten chapters of this epic saga of mystery, betrayal, and finally, triumph, we see how God uses Esther's inner and physical beauty to save the lives of His chosen people, the Israelites. Her story demonstrates how God's purpose unfolds behind the scenes in all of our lives as He works all things out for His ultimate good.

While all cultures, ancient and contemporary, reward beautiful women in many tangible ways, physical beauty often comes at a cost. In Esther's case, her emerging beauty captured the attention of the king's staff, who were commanded to sweep the city and bring back beautiful young women for the king. The previous queen had disrespected her husband, so her crown was removed, and the search for a new queen had begun.

The second chapter of Esther's story documents the process of preparing these young women to meet the king. Since the king was the top man in the land, his staff prepared the women to meet the king's high standards. We might be shocked at the lengths that celebrities employ to look glamorous, but many of their strategies could be considered elementary compared to what Esther and the other candidates experienced. Some of those beauty treatments included six months of massages with oil and six months of cosmetic treatments. Now, I don't know about you, but after twelve months of daily spa treatments and the best foods, I'd probably look pretty good.

We don't know how Esther felt about being taken from her home and entered into an ancient Persian version of *The Bachelor*, but we do know that Mordecai told Esther to keep her Jewish heritage undercover. Chances are, Esther felt uncertain. She had been taken from two homes at a young age, and now she lived in a harem of women in the running to be queen. Complicating matters even more was the fact that King Ahasuerus had a reputation as a brutal man. If there were camera crews back then, Esther would have totally gotten her own reality show out of this!

Yet we also discover that there is something special about Esther in 2:9: "Hegai was very impressed with Esther and treated her kindly. He quickly ordered a special menu for her and provided her with beauty treatments. He also assigned her seven maids specially chosen from the king's palace, and he moved her and her maids into the best place in the harem."

It seems that Esther's inner qualities attracted the attention of the king's chief eunuch in charge of preparing the maidens. If Esther was loud, rude, demanding, or bratty, chances are Hegai wouldn't give her the time of day. However, we see how Esther's inner beauty carried favor.

One of those beautiful inner qualities, gentleness, is apparent early in the story: "When it was Esther's turn to go to the king, she accepted the advice of Hegai, the eunuch in charge of the harem. She asked for nothing except what he suggested, and she was admired by everyone who saw her" (2:15).

Like Abigail whom I mentioned earlier in chapter 12, Esther possessed a humility that garnered favor from those who could have harmed her.

In the next chapters, we read that Esther captivated the king and that he crowned her as queen. If this was just a story about a beautiful woman becoming queen, Esther would be quickly forgotten in history.

Evil and ugly shows up in the form of a man named Haman. There is a lot of backstory on Haman and his ancestry, but the short version is that Haman descended from people who hated the Jewish people. One day, Haman and Moredecai faced off, and after the altercation, Haman plotted to eliminate the Jewish people. He used his power and position to elicit the king's participation in setting up a planned massacre.

THE POWER OF INNER BEAUTY

Mordecai discovered Haman's plot and told Esther. Her first reaction was to use the it's-not-my-problem card. Then, Mordecai reminded Esther that her head could roll off her shoulders just like the others if the planned massacre took place.

Esther's physical beauty wasn't going to save her life. If we put all of our effort into pursuing physical beauty, we aren't going to have what it takes when the pressure cranks up in our lives. When tragedy strikes or when relationships run off course, long eyelashes and the perfect outfit don't mean a thing. A woman whose mind is preoccupied with physical beauty will collapse under the strain.

Inner beauty gives us the courage to walk with conviction instead of giving ourselves over to what feels right in the moment or reacting out of fear. Inner beauty explains the decision to display kindness over anger or the decision to display humility when snarky-ness or disrespectfulness might feel better in the moment.

Esther girded herself for an unplanned and potentially deadly encounter with the king. In the face of uncertainty, she accepted whatever
might happen while attempting to save her people's lives: "And then,
though it is against the law, I will go in to see the king. If I must die, I
must die" (4:16).

If the king was just attracted to Esther's physical features, she probably would have been killed for approaching unannounced. There
were lots of beautiful women hanging around the palace, and any one
of them could assume the queen's crown. So, why didn't the king kill
Esther? It goes without saying that the providence of God was at work.
But could it be because the king was attracted to Esther's inner beauty?
I think so.

As you read about Esther's appearance before the king as well as
the subsequent gatherings, take note of Esther's gentle and quiet manner on display. Even as she confronted Haman, the man who deftly
arranged the planned slaughter of an entire race of her people, Esther
displayed the qualities of inner beauty that no doubt saved her people
in the end. When the time was right, Esther spoke to the king with
passion and conviction, and he believed her over the man that was
second-in-command of his kingdom. That, ladies, is the power of inner
beauty on display.

Haman's plot was foiled, and he was executed. Esther's inner and
outer beauty was used by God to save the Jewish people.

STRIKING YOUR BEAUTY BALANCE

When you look at the diagram of the beauty balance, does it make
sense? I'm sure you want to strike the right balance, but what does that
look like in your life?

Some of you are wondering how you can know when you've got the
right balance. Proverbs 31:25-26 describes the ideal beauty balance:
"She is clothed with strength and dignity, and she laughs without fear

of the future. When she speaks, her words are wise, and she gives instructions with kindness."

Proverbs 31 contains a mother's instruction to her son regarding the type of woman to choose as a wife. This chapter contains admonitions pertaining to inner and physical beauty, culminating in Proverbs 31:30: "Charm is deceptive, and beauty does not last; but a woman who fears the LORD will be greatly praised."

God uses Proverbs 31 to show that a complete woman isn't perfect; rather, she understands her priorities. She understands proportional balance.

Our Proverbs 31 woman beckons us to follow her toward the magnificent reward of reflecting the beauty of God's character in our lives. When we display attitudes, beliefs, and character that are consistent with God's beautiful nature, we mirror strength and beauty that not only honor God but also draw others to us.

My dear sister, my prayer for you is contained within Proverbs 31:25-26, that you would walk in strength and dignity and possess an inner beauty that radiates out for our world to see.

CONCLUSION

My friend, we're at the end of this journey. It has been a privilege. You've allowed me to share my life and stories with you. My prayer is that, at many times during the course of reading this book, you and God have been able to do business. That as you have identified your beauty narratives and you've grappled with the parts of your body that you hate, my prayer is that at some point you've gained a small glimpse of new beauty. I hope that as you look in the mirror, you've begun to challenge the negative words that you say about your appearance. Most of all, I hope that you might have even whispered the words: *I am beautiful.* That would be such an answer to my prayer. Of course, it would be exactly what God desires for you as well.

NOTES

1. Our Ugly Struggle with Beauty
1. Dr. Nancy Etcoff, Dr. Susie Orbach, Dr. Jennifer Scott, and Heidi D'Agostino, "The Real Truth About Beauty: A Global Report: Findings of the Global Study of Women, Beauty and Well-Being," commissioned by Dove, a Unilever Beauty Brand, September 2004, www .clubofamsterdam.com/contentarticles/52%20Beauty/dove_white _paper_final.pdf.
2. Dictionary.com, s.v., "beauty," accessed June 8, 2014, http://dictionary .reference.com/browse/beauty
3. Barbara Roose, personal interview with Anonymous, December 8, 2012.

2. Who Told Us That We Weren't Beautiful?
1. *Ladies Home Journal*, cover, November 2012.
2. Rachel Martin, "Women and Vanity: The Societal Pressures to Look 'Perfect,'" *Indiana News Center*, November 14, 2014, http://www .21alive.com/lifestyle/video/Women-and-Vanity-The-Societal -Pressures-to-Look-Perfect-133851853.html.
3. Barbara Roose, *Created with Curves* survey, SurveyMonkey, October 28, 2012.
4. Ibid.
5. Ibid.
6. See www.DanaCarvey.net.

3. What Is Your Beauty Narrative?
1. *Harper's Bazaar* staff, "Celebrities Talk Beauty," *Harper's Bazaar*, June 18, 2010, www.harpersbazaar.com/beauty/makeup-articles/celebrity -beauty-0610#slide-2.
2. Barbara Roose, *Created with Curves* survey, SurveyMonkey, October 28, 2012.

4. Flaw Finding
1. Barbara Roose, *Created with Curves* survey, SurveyMonkey, October 28, 2012.

2. Ibid.
3. Ibid.
4. Ibid.
5. Ibid.
6. Ibid.
7. Ibid.

5. Beauty's Goodness
1. William Stewart, "Beauty of a Rose," February 2012.

6. Defining "Divine Beauty"
1. Amy Rose Spiegel, "15 Undeniable Style and Beauty Lessons from Miss Piggy," Buzz Feed, September 19, 2013, www.buzzfeed.com /verymuchso/15-undeniable-style-and-beauty-lessons-from-miss -piggy.
2. Barbara Roose, *Created with Curves* survey, SurveyMonkey, October 28, 2012.
3. The quote, "Beauty is in the eye of the beholder," is attributed to many individuals including Plato, Shakespeare, and Margaret Wolfe Hungerford.
4. J. Strong, *Strong's Exhaustive Concordance of the Bible* (Nashville: Abingdon Press, 1980).
5. L. Michaels, T. Fey, M. S. Water , L. Lohan, R. McAdams, T. Meadows, and A. Poehler, *Mean Girls*, directed by Mark Waters (Hollywood, CA: Paramount Pictures, 2004), DVD.
6. R. C. Sproul, *The Holiness of God*, rev. ed. (Carol Stream, IL: Tyndale, 1998).
7. Ibid.

7. See God First
1. "Bullied Girl Voted the Ugliest on the Internet Gives an Amazing Speech," accessed June 8, 2014, www.youtube.com /watch?v=R0OV92Yyl20.
2. Barbara Roose, *Created with Curves* survey, SurveyMonkey, October 28, 2012.
3. J. Strong. *Strong's Exhaustive Concordance of the Bible* (Nashville: Abingdon Press, 1980).

8. What Have I Done to Myself?

1. Barbara Roose, *Created with Curves* survey, SurveyMonkey, October 28, 2012.
2. Henry Cloud and John Townsend, *Boundaries: When to Say Yes, How to Say No to Take Control of Your Life*, rev. ed. (Grand Rapids, MI: Zondervan, 1992).
3. Henry Cloud, "Celebrate Recovery East Coast Summit Training" (conference, Greenville, SC, July 6-9, 2013).
4. Barbara Roose, *Created with Curves* survey, SurveyMonkey, October 28, 2012.
5. Ibid.
6. Ibid.
7. Ibid.

9. Pick Me

1. S. Michael Houdmann, "What Should We Learn from the Life of Jacob?" Godquestions.org, www.gotquestions.org/life-Jacob.html.
2. R. C. Sproul, *The Holiness of God* (Wheaton, IL: Tyndale, 1993).

10. The Vagina Dialogue

1. Barbara Roose, *Created with Curves* survey, SurveyMonkey, October 28, 2012.
2. Barbara Roose, personal interview with Dr. Susan Pohlod, December 12, 2013.

11. God's Paint Palette

1. *Joy of Painting with Bob Ross*, directed by Sally Schenck (New York: Public Broadcasting Station, 1984–94).
2. Associated Press, "British Parents Give Birth to Second Pair of One-in-a-Million Twins—One Black, One White," *NY Daily News*, January 2, 2009, www.nydailynews.com/news/world/british-parents-give-birth-pair-one-in-a-million-twins-black-white-article-1.421824.
3. Todd Wood, "Four Women, a Boat, and Lots of Kids: A Reevaluation of Mitochondrial Eve," *Answers Magazine*, February 13, 2008, www.answersingenesis.org/articles/am/v3/n2/four-women-boat-kids.
4. Barbara Roose, *Created with Curves* survey, SurveyMonkey, October 28, 2012.

12. Cultivating Our Inner Beauty

1. Martin H. Manser, ed., *Dictionary of Bible Themes*.
2. There is not a copyrighted source, but credit is given to Socrates's Three Sieves for inspiring the idea of the T.H.I.N.K acronym.

13. Stand Tall

1. Elliott Almond, "Fallen Giant: Visiting Dyerville in Humbolt Redwoods," *San Jose Mercury News*, June 18, 2011, www.mercurynews.com/ci_18289522.

14. God Don't Like Ugly

1. According to Redd Foxx, "Beauty may be skin deep, but ugly goes clear to the bone."
2. Charles R. Swindoll, "The Freedom of Forgiving," *Insight for Living Ministries*, www.insight.org/resources/articles/encouragement-healing/freedom-of-forgiving.html?l=forgiveness.

15. What We'll Give Away for Love

1. Barbara Roose, personal interview, December 7, 2013.

16. Just Like Eyebrows, Two Are Better Than One

1. Barbara Roose, *Created with Curves* survey, SurveyMonkey, October 28, 2012.
2. Ibid.
3. *National Geographic*, "Porcupine": *National Geographic.com*, http://animals.nationalgeographic.com/animals/mammals/porcupine.

17. Healing from the Inside Out

1. "History of Feminine Hygiene Products," accessed December 2013, http://menstrualcup.co/history-menstrual-products/.
2. Heather Farrell, "Woman with an Issue of Blood," *Women in the Scriptures*, April 16, 2012, www.womeninthescriptures.com/2012/04/woman-with-issue-of-blood.html.
3. Dr. James Dobson, "God's Sovereignty," radio broadcast with Dr. Richard Swenson, 2005.

18. If the Barn Needs Paintin'

1. Brené Brown, presentation at TEDxHouston, October 6, 2010, https://www.youtube.com/watch?v=X4Qm9cGRub0&feature=kp.

2. Henry Cloud and John Townsend, *Boundaries: When to Say Yes, How to Say No to Take Control of Your Life*, rev. ed. (Grand Rapids, MI: Zondervan, 1992).

3. Kari Morgan, "The Fine Line between Nice and Doormat: Setting Boundaries," March 14, 2011,www.thekathleenshow.com/2011/03/14/dr-henry-cloud-transcript.

19. Becoming a Woman Who C.A.R.E.S.

1. Andy Stanley, "What's Your Bowl of Stew?"(Catalyst Conference, Atlanta, GA, October 7, 2010).

2. Lysa TerKeurst, *Made to Crave* (Grand Rapids, MI: Zondervan, 2010).

20. Balancing Inner and Physical Beauty

1. Felicia Fonseca, "Skywire: Nik Wallenda Completes 1,500-Foot High-Wire Walk Near Grand Canyon Live on Discovery Channel," *Huffington Post*, June 23, 2103, www.huffingtonpost.com/2013/06/23/skywire-nik-wallenda_n_3488161.html.